PUGLIA WITH THE GLOVES OFF

Book One

SALENTO

Richard Walmsley

Author of eight novels – all set in Italy
The Puglia series:
Dancing to the Pizzica *(2012)*
The Demise of Judge Grassi *(2013)*
Leonardo's Trouble with Molecules *(2014)*
+
The Case of the Sleeping Beauty *(2015)*
(A Commissario Stancato novel – set in Abruzzo)

A Close Encounter with Mushrooms *(2016)*
(A second case for Commissario Beppe Stancato)

The Vanishing Physicist *(2017)*

(Commissario Beppe Stancato's third case)

Death is Buried *(2020)*
(A fourth case for Beppe Stancato)

The Curse of Collemaga   *(2019)*
(A free-standing mystery novel set in Abruzzo)

+

*And a collection of humorous and unusual short stories
entitled*
'Long Shorts' *(2010 – 2016)*

al mio grande amico /
nemico !!
Jonathan .

*The front cover is a photograph of Gallipoli taken by
the author and adapted by Natalia – who has now turned 19
and is at University studying graphic design.*

Buona lettura!

Richard.

(29/10/21)

Introduction

Never been to Puglia? Thinking of visiting this part of Italy? I lived there for nearly nine years between 2001 and 2009. Now I am regretting that I ever came back to the barely-United Kingdom of 2019. I miss the warmth, the food, the idiosyncratic ways of its people, the hospitality, the deviousness of market-stall holders, the smells, the sound and sight of people of all ages united on their local town squares joining in their local folk dance – the *Pizzica* - whose rhythms will haunt me until the day I die. Not to mention the fresh fruit and vegetables and the abundance of healthy dishes which almost guarantee longevity – if not quite eternal life.

My nine life-changing years entitle me to tell you the way it is in this far-flung region of Italy. All will be revealed. Nothing will be concealed. No other book on Puglia will be quite the same as this one. This is *'Puglia with the gloves off'*.

R.W.

1:   *First impressions...*

Flying into Brindisi Airport has become one of my most treasured memories of the 21st century. I inevitably have the sensation that I have returned home. The plane from London has taken about two and a half hours to reach the heel of Italy. It usually follows the Adriatic coastline all the way down from Ancona and then flies into 'Salento Airport' as it is now called. The plane glides a few feet over the usually turquoise blue sea and skims above olive groves and low, white buildings before depositing the passengers at the bright, lively terminal which smells of espresso coffee and slices of hot pizza – plus that *je ne sais quoi* sensation which pervades the atmosphere in any Mediterranean country.

Salento is the region which stretches south from Brindisi, through the provincial capital, Lecce, right down to Santa Maria di Leuca at the very tip of Italy's 'heel'. If your destination is further to the north of Puglia, you might well fly into Bari instead of Brindisi.

It is quite logical to fly to Bari, I suppose. After all, it *is* Puglia's biggest city and is situated almost exactly half way up the lengthy Pugliese coastline. Until you study a map of the whole of Italy and calculate it for yourself, you would scarcely credit the fact that, by travelling from the southernmost tip of Puglia up to its boundary with Molise, its nearest coastal neighbour, you will already have covered one third of the whole length of the Italian peninsula. Puglia is very long.

Escaping from Puglia – which you might want to do on occasions – is akin to overcoming the pull of the Earth's gravitational force. It will take three hours by express train to accomplish your reluctant get-away. The Intercity service, which confusingly used to be called *Eurostar* but has now been renamed *La Freccia Bianca (The White Arrow)*, will take a further seven hours to reach Milano, its final destination in the distant northern realms of Italy. There is also *La Freccia Bianca* intercity service from Lecce to Torino as an alternative to Milano. Travelling to this remote destination takes about eleven hours to accomplish. But by then, you have almost reached France, which begins to sound as if you are nearer England. Italy is narrow but very long. Italian railway engineers have had to cope with a much more arduous task than most other nations, Italy's geological make-up being what it is. They have either had to drive their railways through mountains to get from one side of the country to the other – or squeeze the track into a narrow corridor between sea and mountains, as is the case with the line which runs down the Adriatic coast – on the 'wrong' side of Italy. By 'wrong' I simply mean the less familiar eastern side whose delights remain largely undiscovered by the majority of foreign tourists.

Puglia is very much on the map nowadays. It deserves to be, I suppose, because it depends more and more on tourism to scrape a living economically speaking. Many foreigners decide to live out their lives in Puglia, or at least buy a summer property down there; Helen Mirren for one – not to mention Meryl Streep. So Puglia really must have something out-of-the-ordinary going for it. George Clooney favoured Abruzzo – higher up on the opposite side of Italy to Rome, where his film 'The American' was shot.

When I first went down to Lecce, at the outset of this century, Ryanair only flew as far south as Pescara, in Abruzzo, obliging one to take the train for the rest of the way. On my first such journey, I was amazed to discover on looking out of the rear carriage window that, on leaving Brindisi behind, the train rattled along on a *single-track* railway. I seriously wondered if I had somehow been transported into another dimension and that I was now travelling through the African Savannah. There didn't seem to be any giraffes in the fields so I assumed I might still be in the right country – and century.

In the early years of the twenty-first century, this part of southern Puglia finally got a twin track railway down to Lecce. The single line track, ordered by Mussolini, was replaced by a modern one so that trains could flash past each other as they do almost everywhere else in Europe. But this observation does bring home to one how recent this part of Puglia's admittance to the modern world has been. Suddenly, the jewel in Puglia's baroque crown, Lecce, is on the tourist map. Usually, becoming famous is nigh on disastrous. Just look at Venice! But since Lecce has become a tourist destination, European money has been modestly poured into its coffers. The city has had a real face-lift and brought a cautious but patchy degree of prosperity to it which was lacking until the 21st Century got underway.

Not all the inhabitants of Lecce approve of the arrival of tourists from all over the world. Graffiti bearing the words 'Tourists are bleeding Salento dry' and many such variations on a theme can be spotted spray-canned on hoardings on the outskirts of the city. The situation has not degenerated, as it has in Venice, to the point where tourists are fed, watered and herded on unsmilingly to their next destination.

I had, as fate decreed it, acquired a teaching job in unknown Lecce and ended up staying in and around this city for nearly nine years. I sometimes flew into Bari rather than Brindisi – even later on – simply because I could catch a direct coach down to 'my' village, Sannicola, well to the south of Lecce, where I began to put down tenuous roots.

Taking the *navetta* from the airport to Bari station, where I could catch my coach down south, I quickly became very grateful that I did not have to live in Bari. On one of the early journeys on the airport bus, we lumbered through the outskirts of Bari past a wilderness of high-rise flats, bleak patches of scrubland and an unfinished railway line, consisting of a long stretch of transparent plastic tunnel through which the train was intended to run. Nobody seemed quite sure where the unfinished railway line was supposed to go. At one point of our bus journey to the city centre, we passed a burnt-out newspaper kiosk on the pavement.

'Ah,' exclaimed one of the passengers to the others, 'he obviously didn't pay his *pizzo!*' I had to look up the word in my dictionary because it sounded as if it must mean something to eat topped with tomato sauce and mozzarella. Or maybe I had simply misheard the pronunciation. But no, I discovered, the word *pizzo* means 'protection money paid to the mafia clans'. It was my first introduction to the seedier side of life in Southern Italy. Mercifully, such signs of the underworld, which exists in an almost invisible parallel universe, do not often intrude into daily life. Unless, that is, you are a shopkeeper or a newspaper kiosk owner - or if you should happen to go out of your way to provoke the many-tentacled beast in its lair. A local mayor in a coastal town called Ugento did just that, while I was living in Sannicola. He was unceremoniously assassinated, leaving his wife a widow and his children fatherless - all this, simply because, one can assume, he had refused to grant building permission to the local mafia *boss* and presumably had turned down the back-hander that would have accompanied such an illicit request for cooperation. Illegal edifices are commonplace in Southern Italy. They are called *'abusivo'* in Italian – 'abusive buildings'. What a delightful turn of phrase! Incidentally, the Italians often refer to the mafia as *La Piovra* – The Octopus – especially the Sicilian mafia, *Cosa Nostra.*

But you should not let such sinister undercurrents cloud your judgement of Puglia as a whole. It has an ancient magic all of its own, which precedes modern day evils by centuries. Puglia will beguile and seduce you for the rest of your life. Much of Puglia's charm lies simply in its seeming reluctance to adapt to the modern world in which it accidentally finds itself. For starters – be prepared for this – they don't really speak Italian down there if they can avoid it.

Mind you, it would be a mistake to assume that there is a universal language called Italian spoken in the rest of the Peninsula. When we pick up our BBC Italian course books to learn the language two or three steps removed from the reality which is Italy, it is tempting to believe that our efforts

7

enable us to share the charm and romanticism of this country. In point of fact, the linguistic situation is far more complex than we imagine. Official 'Italian' is purportedly based on a traditional Florentine dialect. But separate and distinct dialects abound depending on where you are staying. Usually, they are variations of recognisable Italian. However, in the case of Bergamo – a beautiful town just to the north east of Milano – and its surrounding countryside, they do not speak a dialect! Surprised? You should be! Because they speak another language altogether, called *Bergamasco.*

While I was living in Sannicola, I was astounded to discover from a RAI 1 TV documentary that *'49% of Italians now speak the Italian language at home.'* This statement was proclaimed as a sign of the 'progress' that education and the mass media had achieved.

'Hang on a minute,' I said to myself. 'This means that 51% of the population still speak something other than 'standard' Italian when left to their own devices.' It was a startling revelation at the time. Maybe the percentage has crept up a bit by now. But this still amounts to about half the population whose first instinct is to communicate with each other in a dialect. In point of fact, whilst teaching school kids, I noticed that as soon as they left the classroom, they would immediately revert to talking to each other in dialect. The fact is that 'Italian' - as we think we know it - is a language that has been superimposed on the population since the historically recent unification of this very young and disparate nation.

The dialect spoken in the southernmost part of Puglia, around and below the city of Lecce, is called *Salentino* – just like its people. It does not respect the official boundaries of Puglia at all. The *Salentino* dialect stretches westwards across the Peninsula and into Sicily, undergoing local variations as it travels west. A person from Salento will have little difficulty understanding a Sicilian speaking in *his* dialect. But travel up to Bari and just listen to the natives speaking *their* local dialect – *Barese.* Nobody who is not from Bari can understand it at all.

In the village of Sannicola, where I lived for six years, there is a talented family group of musicians, surname *Giaffreda,* who sing Salentino folk music. The group calls itself *Schiattacore* – a dialect word meaning 'Heartbreak'. They have recorded two CDs of their haunting, traditional music. Their latest release is accompanied by a little booklet with the words of the songs printed out. There is a translation of the words in smaller print beneath each song – in Italian. This is - it must be obvious by now - because the songs are sung largely in their own dialect.

That is not all, however. Two of the songs on the second CD are from a local town to the south of Lecce called CALIMERA. Does that word ring any bells? Yes, it sounds like the Greek word for 'good morning'. This is because the locals speak a dialect called, unbelievably, GRIKO. Calimera was, once upon a time, a Greek settlement. I mention all this simply to make the point that the linguistic undercurrents in Italy are immensely complex. But don't worry! The natives - apart from some who were born before WW2 – are all bilingual. They will speak to you in an Italian that you should be able to decipher with a bit of concentration. In point of fact, the people of Salento speak Italian with a clear accent – until they revert to dialect, in which nearly every word seems to end with a 'u' sound! And they might say *Bon di* instead of *Buon giorno.*

My first port of call, way back in the dawn of the 21st Century, was Lecce. I had acquired an English teaching post in a private language school, grandly called 'The Oxford Institutes'. The name was designed to entice the locals to attend English courses thanks to its prestigious sounding association with our oldest university. No copyright problems to prevent this happening, obviously. This explains the plethora of similar language school names which abound in Italy: The Cambridge Institutes, The Milton Academy or The Byron School of English. But imaginations have really run riot in the Italian peninsula as a whole, with even wilder-sounding names such as The Red Bus Company and The Sherlock Holmes Language College. All in a desperate bid to sound as authentically English as possible – or so they believe.

The most obvious starting point for a book which purports to reveal the secrets of Puglia must be the magnificent city of Lecce. I was due to attend an induction course at the Oxford Institutes the following week, before taking up my teaching post in a town called Casarano, fifty kilometres to the south of Lecce. The Oxford Institutes had just opened a branch in this small semi-rural, semi-industrial town of just over 20 000 inhabitants. The production of olive oil is its main industry. But when I first went down there, they manufactured shoes, socks and clothing. A company, ingeniously but enigmatically calling itself *Meltin'pot*, manufacturing jeans and other articles of clothing, has just about survived the severe economic crisis. Much of the other industries have migrated to Romania – or even further afield - leaving a gaping hole in the town's economy.

After brief introductions to the school's managers and teachers, I was deposited on that Friday afternoon in a local hotel no more than 500 metres from the School. I was left to my own devices until the following Monday morning.

In point of fact, I felt abandoned, as you tend to feel when you have just arrived in a strange city, cut off from everybody and everything that is familiar. I considered escaping back to the comfort of my own home or, at the very least, back up to my more customary haunts in the distant north of the peninsula. Down here in the Deep South, relatively speaking a mere stone's throw away from Africa, everything felt alien. Before my departure, I had been issued with dire warnings from well-meaning Italian friends from Bologna and Milan that I should expect to be shocked by the cultural abyss which exists between the North and the South. Naturally, I had blithely dismissed these assertions as stemming from the well-known prejudices of northern Italians towards their distant cousins in the south. Such a divide does exist. I'm not convinced that it warrants the word 'abyss' though!

The differences are not always that obvious; after all, there are still motorcars bombing around rather than donkey-drawn carts. And normal people pay for goods with credit cards. Like all Italians, the natives of Puglia are inordinately attached to their mobile phone devices. But the realisation you have landed in a different world steals up on you over a period of time. You are lulled into a comfortable sense of security before you begin to perceive that you have been beguiled by the subtle magic of another land and culture altogether.

I managed to shake off the feelings of encroaching isolation on that first day in Lecce and forced myself to leave the security of my hotel room. I asked at the reception desk how to get to the city centre.

'You can't miss it, *signore,*' they told me, smiling indulgently at my ignorance, whilst gesticulating vaguely somewhere beyond the confines of the reception area. 'Would you like us to call you a taxi?' they offered.

'Is it that far?' I asked surprised. I still had to learn, as I would over the next few months, that Italians *never* walk anywhere if they can avoid it. Wearing out shoe leather seems to constitute a greater financial strain on their family budgets than wearing down the tread of motor car tyres.

As I walked towards what I hoped was the historical centre of Lecce, I could see the top of the lofty *Campanile del Duomo* towering above the other buildings. The cathedral bell tower seemed quite a long way away but served as a guide to tell me I was walking in roughly the right direction. It was all trial and error at this stage. My first discovery about Lecce was that the old part of the city is still largely surrounded by an ancient stone wall. I wasn't to know that I was taking the long way round, but it did not matter since I had nearly three whole days in which to get lost.

I discovered a park which had an elaborate fountain as big as a small swimming pool, flower beds, statues of the venerable ancestors of Lecce, lawns and trees in great profusion. The grass was green and carefully tended and, as usual on the continent, it was forbidden to walk on it. Notices sprouted out of the lawns at various points announcing imperiously *Non calpestare le aiuole.* That was two new Italian words I learnt on my first day - *calpestare,* meaning to tread on someone else's preserve and *aiuole,* meaning lawns, herbaceous borders or flower-beds. Only Italian, of all the European languages, could boast a six-letter word like that with only one consonant in it. I practised saying it and came to the conclusion that Italians must get tired out talking all day long, by the time my lips and mouth had gone through the verbal gymnastics of practising the pronunciation of *EYE-YOU-WOLLÉ* a dozen times – the word for lawns etc.

There was an archway in the city wall just opposite the park. After a kilometre's walk round the busy ring road, I had finally found a way of entering the old part of town. That was the point in time when my love of Lecce began. There is hardly a stone in the whole city centre which does not breathe the word 'history' down every street and in every *piazza.* The most recent architecture dates from Mussolini's fascist era – of which, more later. I spent the afternoon wandering around with my mouth open in amazement. No wonder friends had raved about it before my departure. They were not exaggerating. The *campanile* is set to one side of the spacious *Piazza del Duomo*. At sixty-eight metres, this bell tower is apparently among the tallest in Europe. The cathedral square is simply imposing. I mean it is imposing and simple at the same time. The inside of the *Duomo*, darkly baroque, echoes with the footsteps of nuns, priests, devout old ladies and a few Italian sightseers. But it was another building that I fell in love with immediately. Huge wooden doors set in a magnificent stone façade lead into the courtyard of the *Museo Diocesano dell'Arte Sacra* - the Diocesan Museum of Sacred Art. I walked round the flagstone courtyard. An ancient and ornate stone well sat in the centre of a small, rectangle of lawn. Lemon trees with January fruit like bright yellow light bulbs were hanging from their branches in the warm sunshine. The lawn was, of course, of the 'forbidden' variety, but I skipped across it regardless to peer down into the depths of the well. Some official called out something to the effect that I shouldn't be there so I pretended I couldn't understand Italian. He shrugged his shoulders and gave up.

I felt drawn to return to the city centre and the *Piazza del Duomo* after dark the following day. It was lit up as if by magic and looked even more enchanting than in the daylight.

15

The streets were full of families, lively but perfectly civilised teenagers, cyclists, nuns and priests all out for their evening *passeggiata*. Even the patrolling policemen seemed to be joining in too. I had been told about this very Italian habit of going for a stroll along the streets and around the *piazze* just before nightfall. The tradition of the *passeggiata* is still very much alive – and even more so in the deep south of Italy. I realise that this statement seems to contradict what I said earlier about Italians preferring not to walk. So, I had better amend my original statement. When it is a matter of getting from point A to point B, Italians prefer not to walk. But when there is absolutely no other purpose than to wander around aimlessly in order to be seen in public, then it is fine to wear out shoe leather. I suspect they all possess special shoes just for the occasion. I was struck by the fact that a lot of the strollers were groups of girls not even properly into their teens. Was it a sign of lax parenting? No. I had just managed to identify what it was that I was feeling as I joined in the general *mêlée* for the first time; it was a sense of security which I would not have felt walking around London after dark. Lecce felt good! I can't vouch for the safety of the city in the early hours – *le ore piccole* – because I was inevitably fast asleep by then.

2:   Lecce: 'All the city's a stage...'

When I arrived in Lecce at the beginning of this century, Italy had not yet been blessed – or inflicted - with the euro. Although my one million lire monthly wages sounded like a fortune, it was in reality a very modest sum indeed. Having to pay 2000 lire for a pizza seemed like the height of extravagance. Nowadays, you still pay a mere €5 – or less - for a pizza. Unfortunately, when you work it out with a calculator, you realise just how cheap life was in those long gone, pre-euro days. The cost of everything has virtually doubled. The average earnings of normal Italians are still trying to catch up. Most people at the time accused the shopkeepers of blatant profiteering. For us Brits, used to paying over the odds for everything under the sun, parting with a mere €5 for a platter-sized, wood-oven-baked pizza oozing with stringy mozzarella seems like a brilliant deal – which it is, of course. In fact, if you are careful, everything you buy or service you pay for should fall into this category even today; especially in the less affluent South. I am obliged to add a post-Brexit caveat at this point. It *was* a brilliant deal until the Pound Sterling shrunk by over 15%. Euro-Sterling seems to be permanently set around the parity mark at the time of adding this sentence – four years after I began writing this account.

Car hire can be costly if only because of the high insurance premiums in this part of the world – but not so high in Puglia as it is in Naples, I'm told.

You should be prudent, however; don't hesitate to query prices if you think you are being overcharged. It helps to speak a little Italian. But it is often enough to look as if you intend to put up a fight to make the hardiest shopkeeper or market-stall holder back down. Then they will smile charmingly and blame the electronic mind of the cash till for the error – and all will be sweetness and light between you. Be a little wary of vegetable and cheese sellers in the markets – they are fond of giving you more than you asked for. While your tomatoes or *Provolone* are still on the weighing scales, they will smile and say 'It's a bit over half a kilo – shall I take some off for you?' That puts the onus on you because you don't want to be seen to be penny-pinching. When you check on the weight later, you find it's nearer a kilo. However, I can truthfully say that the majority of restaurant owners, shopkeepers and hoteliers are honest enough and will only take what is due to them – give or take a euro or two. Since Mario Monti was in charge of Italy, every shopkeeper or stall-holder is legally obliged to issue you with a receipt. If they don't, it means they are avoiding paying VAT. In the current situation -2020 – every Italian is encouraged to pay for even a cup of espresso coffee by credit card, simply to avoid the perennial problem of tax-dodging. By the way, it is rare to pay much over €1 for a cup of espresso coffee; cf Britain, where you will pay nearly double for the same dose of coffee.

Although the euro has been a mixed blessing in Italy, it has benefited Lecce in many ways. After something like a twenty-year delay, funds arrived to complete their ring road – *la tangenziale* – which has taken a lot of heavy traffic away from the city. Not that you would notice. It all looks pretty hectic during rush hour. And a lot of the lorries were heading for Lecce anyway. But driving a car through Lecce's historic centre and parking there is, thankfully, restricted to a limited number of permit holders.

The streets used to be in sore need of resurfacing. The main streets in the *centro storico* have been conscientiously re-cobbled in traditional fashion. The magnificent bell tower – *il campanile* – together with all the breathtakingly ornate facades of the city's baroque churches were looking a bit grubby. Now they have all been sand-blasted to cleanliness. They gleam in the meridian sunlight, in honour of the growing number of tourists of all nationalities who are discovering the hidden treasure that is Lecce.

When you walk around some of the narrower old streets, off the tourist trail, one discovers that funds did not quite stretch to repairing the back-streets and alleyways. Patches of tarmac try desperately to cover the original, uneven cobble stones, designed to allow you to sprain an unwary ankle or unseat cyclists.

But no matter! It is the side streets where you find the best eating places in town and where the real people of this city have their homes. In the early days, I lived down one such alleyway for a whole year. It went under the fascinating name of *Vico Storto Carità Vecchia.* Translated, that means roughly speaking: *The Crooked Alley of the Old Charity.*

Well, it didn't mean much to me either – especially when translated into English. I subsequently learnt to my amusement that the 'Old Charity' in question was nothing more complicated than the availability of certain ladies who provided an outlet for men's pent up libidos. At the outset of the twenty-first century, there was only one remaining mature lady living in the house next door to me. She provided for the needs of a handful of discreet, ageing clients. She was indeed a very charitable, kindly soul, who took a mild interest in the presence of her displaced Englishman. The alleyway where I lived is still there – next to a luxurious hotel and just opposite the magnificent stone edifice belonging to the *Banca d'Italia.* That is what is so appealing about Lecce; the ancient and modern, the rich and the poor, co-exist in intimate proximity.

By the time I arrived, in 2001, the prostitutes had moved 'downtown'. In the case of Lecce, which is a city on a very human scale, this meant about a five-or-six minutes' walk towards *La Porta San Biagio.* In the great, new scheme of things, the honourable councillors of Lecce decided to remove all obvious signs of these good ladies – plus one colourful and ubiquitous transsexual. No more surreptitious peering into the gaudy, ground floor interiors of the ladies' dens through their lace-curtained French windows as you passed furtively by. Nowadays, such transactions are carried out via mobile phones. *Le ragazze squillo* – as call girls are referred to – carry on in discreet apartments dotted about the city; a loss of one bit of local colour, in my opinion. Today, a number of the Brazilian and African girls line the lanes running along the *superstrada* which leads to Gallipoli and ply their trade in public view. Not nearly such a discreet solution as before, I would suggest. Nobody in authority seems in too much of a hurry to have them removed. This phenomenon is commonplace throughout Italy, by the way. I am not singling out Puglia.

Now back to our all-important tour of Lecce. The beautiful thing about Lecce is its size. It is easy to walk from one side of its historic centre to the other in a leisurely hour or so. A large part of the *centro storico* is still surrounded by its ancient wall, as I said before. There are three historic gateways into the city: *La Porta Napoli, La Porta Rudiae* and *La Porta San Biagio*. They are each architectural masterpieces in their own right. One can wander at leisure through the old centre of Lecce, feasting one's eyes on stunning architectural buildings every step of the way. I have always had the impression that walking round Italian cities is akin to witnessing a theatrical performance in progress. The stage sets and props are extravagant works of art. Lecce, I feel, gives this impression more than any Italian city I have visited. In eight years living in Salento, I never grew tired of walking round Lecce, night or day, wondering at the imposing magic of its churches and even many of its secular buildings. You simply won't believe your eyes as you wander through its ancient streets. The impression of being caught up in a theatrical event is heightened when you realise that the elaborately carved facades of the baroque churches are quite flat – just like stage scenery. They are make-belief edifices of enormous complexity that fool the eye into believing in the amazing solidity of the city. In point of fact, the buildings are made of Lecce stone. It is ochre in colour, like sand. It is a relatively soft, grainy stone that tends to crumble easily. How does the city manage to survive the centuries so perfectly preserved? It's a mystery!

I have to say that I am the kind of person who is quite content to enter an ancient church or courtyard with the simple aim of staring in wonder at the works of man devoted to our invisible deity over the centuries. If I decide to delve into the origins of an historic building, it will only be after I have visited it. A concise description of each of Lecce's churches can be found on permanent plaques displayed outside each church. This information is usually enough for me. You should find an English version too – all too often translated by an Italian undergraduate who has been studying English for a couple of years - students are cheaper than professional translators who, it must be said, do not always make that much better a job of it. To put it politely, the translations are often rather too literal to make much sense. Italian prose is full of heady, flowery language set in long sentences, which just doesn't sound like good old practical Anglo-Saxon. If you learn but a little about the church's history then at least you can experience first-hand the reality of the cultural gap that exists between an Italian and English way of expressing abstract notions.

I am not going to make a list of the all the churches in Lecce that you should visit. The truth is they *all* deserve to be visited. But if you are on a tight time schedule, you simply cannot afford to miss out on *La Santa Croce (The Holy Cross)* or the church of *San Matteo (Saint Matthew)* and, it goes without saying, the *Duomo,* its *Piazza* and the lofty bell tower. The bell tower can be seen from various parts of the city. It looks like an imposing baroque space rocket poised to take off into the skies above, ready to transport the seeds of European civilisation to other galaxies.

San Matteo is striking both inside and out. My second novel, *The Demise of Judge Grassi,* was partly inspired by this church and a young priest who delivered a lively sermon which involved the whole congregation – young and old. But, I have to confess, the priest was 'borrowed' from the cathedral in Gallipoli, which we will come to in a subsequent chapter.

While you are walking round Lecce, admiring the countless churches and wishing you were staying there for longer, you will soon come across the main square – *La Piazza Sant'Oronzo.* Saint Oronzo, a martyred bishop, stands high up on his plinth with his hands raised in blessing on all who pass below. He is Lecce's patron saint. If you are in Lecce near the end of August, you can join in the *festa* in his honour, when the people of Lecce continue to observe their respect and gratitude towards their patron saint for bringing the plague to an end in the distant past. The statue of Sant'Oronzo was a gift from the city of Brindisi; it seems that they had a spare Sant'Oronzo standing around with little to do. The spacious *piazza* is also the site of a perfectly preserved Roman arena. It is so easy to look down on the semi-circular banks of stone seats and imagine the crowds of Romans cheering on the lions feasting on their Christian fodder. The animal pens and the cells where the victims awaited their fate are now exposed to view.

There is also a Roman theatre tucked away in a back street just three minutes' walk from the *Piazza Sant'Oronzo*. It used to be inhabited by stray cats and discarded coke cans, but is still worth more than a casual glance.

Behind all the splendour of *La Piazza Sant'Oronzo*, you will spot with curiosity a stark reminder of Mussolini's fascist era defiantly reminding everybody of this blot on Italy's more recent history. The functional buildings of this sad era are literally grafted on to their historical counterparts. They house a well-known insurance company. But it is surprising how quickly you can dispel their image from your mind by concentrating on the rest of the *piazza* – until, that is, you spot with shock and disbelief, in one corner of the *piazza,* a McDonald's burger bar. What backhander, one wonders, was paid to the honourable councillors of Lecce to persuade them to wreck the architectural harmony of this place with such a horror! Needless to say, the burger bar is full of Italian families, high school students and tourists, all in need of their daily dose of junk food. Sufficient justification for its existence, some might say!

La Piazza Sant'Oronzo is always teeming with pedestrians of all ages: students, school children, old men talking, fashionable women on bikes, all mingling happily with Puglia's unemployed. It has inviting coffee bars dotted all around it and the best-known ice-cream parlour and *pasticceria* in Lecce in a side street just off the *piazza.* It is called *La Gelateria-Pasticceria Natale.* It should be looked at like any other tourist attraction as an example of the delights that the city has to offer. But my guess is that you will not be able to resist going inside to try out its home-made ice cream, chocolate or cakes. Unfortunately for your health, the competition from similar establishments dotted all around Salento is fierce.

Another unusual phenomenon which you will notice as you amble round the city is the frequency with which you come across evidence of the city's renowned artisanal industry; the local craftsmen create fantastic figures made entirely from *cartapesta* – papier mâché. There is a predominance of religious figures as befits this deeply Catholic part of the world. I have not yet seen a figure of Pope Francis, but I bet there is one by now. The figures are often life-sized. I can't see Ryanair allowing you to stow one on board. But it is good just to stand and be amazed at the creative flair displayed by the craftsmen – and women – perpetuating this ancient tradition. There are eight such workshops dotted around the centre of Lecce – plus a *cartapesta* museum near the *giardini pubblici,* the park, which I mentioned in Chapter 1. You will be truly astounded to discover the level of skill which these craftsmen and craftswomen bring to their creations. And they do not, by any means, all belong to the older generation. You will be impressed by the fact that the art of *cartapesta* in Lecce is a living passion; it has little to do with tourism. This is probably the most striking thing about Puglia, Salento certainly, that so many traditions are kept alive, entirely by – and for the sake of - the local people. The same applies to the folk music of Salento, as you will appreciate if you are fortunate enough to arrive in a town or village where a local *festa* is being held.

Since we were enjoying the experience afforded by *La Piazza Sant'Oronzo,* I should direct your attention to Lecce's splendid castle, *Il Castello Carlo V,* which is so close at hand that it will take you less than one minute's walk to reach it up a little side street next to the *Bar Alvino.* Everybody who is anybody stops off and has their morning coffee and croissant on the *terrazza* outside the *Bar Alvino* – despite the proximity of McDonald's. Or maybe the *Bar Alvino* represents a form of cultural protest against that other incongruous culinary invasion. The *Bar Alvino* got there first, however – by many decades.

A croissant, by the way, is called *un cornetto* and may be filled with a cream paste or with *marmellata*, which confusingly means 'jam' in Italian. If you want a plain one, you ask for *un cornetto vuoto (voo-woto)*, which simply means 'empty'. I learnt the word *cornetto* the hard way. I went into a bar and asked for *Un caffè e un cornuto.* The bar –tender and the customers all jeered with great glee. I had just asked for an espresso and a cuckold. It was a salutary reminder of the perils of presuming one can speak another nation's language and get off scot-free.

If you fancy a change – from a 'cuckold' - you should try *un pasticciotto, (Pasti- TCHOTo)*, a speciality of Salento, which looks like a little pie but is filled with a sweet, rich, yellowy cream paste – like the croissants. Far too tempting once you have tried the first one and subsequently become addicted – and they go so well with your *espresso* or *cappuccino.* None of this nonsense, as in coffee bars in England, where you have to make a linguistically contradictory choice between a 'single' or a 'double' espresso; or distinguish between a 'skinny latte' as opposed to one that hasn't been on a diet.

I am too easily distracted by food, of which there is a veritable cornucopia in this part of the world. Up the side street, then, and you are immediately faced with the *castello* in question. I feel I should draw your attention to it because it is, paradoxically, so big that you almost miss it. It blends in so perfectly with the surroundings that one assumes it is part of Lecce's city wall. In addition, there is a busy main road between you and the castle. You don't usually expect to see castles in the middle of bustling traffic. This one was built by Carlo V *(Carlo Quinto - Charles the Fifth)* to protect himself and his entourage from the endless incursions from the Adriatic and the Ionian coasts by the Saracens. The main aim of that nation in the past seemed to be that of slaughtering as many innocent Christians as possible in the most brutal ways imaginable. Has life changed all that much, one wonders? The whole coastline of Salento is dotted with huge, granite watchtowers to give as much warning as possible of the next raid; but more of that when we go to Otranto later on in this narrative.

Before you decide to go inside the *castello,* it is worth while walking in an anticlockwise direction around the castle to see just how massive it is. You will need to cross the busy road to reach it. I would advise you to cross the road on the pedestrian crossing where there are traffic lights. In Italy, the only advantage of crossing roads on marked pedestrian crossings is that you are covered by insurance if you get knocked down by a motorist. There is no guarantee that drivers will stop to let you cross safely. Indeed, I have often known them to execute a neat swerve to avoid having to slow down as you cross the road. In recent years, many drivers seem to have realised what such crossings are for; they actually stop briefly while you scuttle across the road. Italians in general drive their cars with scant regard for the sanctity of human life. They are usually affable and friendly when not behind a steering wheel. But as soon as they are in motion something in their psyche alters.

I developed a personal theory during the nine years I lived amongst the inhabitants of Salento. There appears to be a 'sense-of-the-future' gene missing. When behind the wheel of a car, they seem totally unaware of the possible consequences of their reckless disregard for safety. Nuns and priests are sometimes the worst offenders. I became convinced that they all have an innate faith in their own immunity. The missing 'future gene' extends beyond mere driving. I spent a great deal of time with a beautiful woman from Salento who refused to put petrol in her tank until it had reached the last drop. She would not face up to the simple fact that car engines only function on fuel until the very final moment before it conked out. She had to wait until the present caught up with the future before she could take the practical step of pulling into a petrol station. It was the same with the credit on her mobile phone.

Sorry, yet another digression. You have crossed the road safely. You are in the *Viale XXV Luglio.* I am uncertain why this road should be called 'Twenty-Fifth of July Street.' Ask a local inhabitant - they will be as puzzled as you are. You will see the entrance to the castle, reached by crossing one of the two original draw-bridges, now permanently lowered. There is a tantalisingly alluring view of the castle's magnificent interior – definitely to be visited when you have the time.

Turn left into *Viale G. Marconi.* At least, we know who *he* was – the *real* inventor of the telephone according to Italians. Follow the path down past the imposing stone walls of the castle as far as the *Piazza Libertini.* You will probably be distracted by the more-or-less permanent market, selling mainly clothes, but also by Moroccans selling exotic samples of African paraphernalia which nobody ever seems to buy. It is truly medieval in character – the simple folk outside the king's castle peddling their wares in the shadow of the massive stone walls. The local Italian stall-holders pack up at lunchtime. But the denizens of darkest Africa stay on until dusk, melting away like wraiths, only to rematerialize the following morning - their endless supply of elephants carved out of wood, leather belts, wrist watches, trinkets and baubles laid out on mats on the ground once again.

The exterior walls of the *Castello Carlo V* look solid and imposing, but apart from this, they look like stone walls. By contrast, the interior of the castle is an architectural gem, with its beautiful arched ceilings, long, graceful galleries and spacious courtyards. The stonework has been cleaned and glows with a soft ochre light. The present castle dates from 1539 and replaced an older one. From 1870 until as recently as 1979, it was a military barracks. In 1983, the military authorities donated the castle to the *Comune* of Lecce. Nowadays, it is used as a conference centre and a cultural exhibition centre. It won't cost you an arm and a leg (or an eye of the head, in Italian) to visit the castle when you have a spare half hour. It will confirm your impression that the city of Lecce is a living museum dedicated without distinction to both its Past and its Present.

Just a few steps back down the *Viale XXV Luglio*, is one of Lecce's two theatres, *Il Teatro Politeama Greco.* Once again, you would be forgiven for walking straight past it without noticing it, since it is bang next door to a lurid ice-cream parlour, specialising in yoghurt ice-cream. The 'lurid' is not a comment on their ice-cream, which is first rate, but not quite as good as the *Natale* just round the corner.

You must be beginning to see just what splendid sights there are in Lecce within just a few seconds walk of each other. This theatre puts on dramas and concerts regularly. Its repertoire caters for all tastes. It might not look much from the outside, but step into the foyer – and even the theatre itself if you can – and you will be transported back to the sumptuous days of the Victorian music hall. There are tiers of boxes on both sides – seating more than the central rows of armchairs. The whole décor has had time, money, and above all, love lavished on its restoration. *Il Politeama Greco* vies with its sister theatre, *Il Paisiello,* just round the corner from *La Porta Napoli.* It is worth while trying to bribe your way into either of these theatres, just to have a look inside. They recall the lavish old 'music-hall' theatres in England, which have all but vanished. Alternatively, if you are in Lecce for a day or two, see if you can book a ticket for a show. It might be an incomprehensibly intellectual play by Pirandello. But you could just yawn away the time admiring the setting. Honestly, I am not exaggerating! It takes your breath away to find such opulent interiors which have managed to survive into the 21st Century unscathed.

* * *

Now it is time to get a bit more geographically orientated in Lecce, and possibly think about the all-important matter of where to have lunch or dinner. From the *Banca d'Italia* building, just to the side of the Roman arena, you should find yourself opposite the church of *Santa Chiara* just where *Via Augusto Imperatore* becomes *Via F. d'Aragona.* Please say *'ciao'* to *Vico Storto* for me, if you even notice it, before you begin descending *Via d'Aragona*, calling in at *La Chiesa Santa Chiara* if it's open. This narrow street goes gently downhill past a variety of eating places and bars, looking very empty at lunchtime but thronging with young people when darkness falls. After a couple of minutes' stroll, you will reach the church of *San Matteo* on your left. Savour the experience of looking inside the church until after you have walked downhill to the first 'entrance gate' to the city, *La Porta San Biagio* – just to get your bearings. It will only take you a couple of minutes.

Step out on to the *Piazza d'Italia* and look back at the *Porta Biagio* from the outside. The audience should view the stage scenery from this perspective. If you look up along the busy *Viale Francesco Lo Re*, you can see the castle again at the top of the road. It is impossible to get lost in Lecce if you keep to the main arteries. To get a picture of the city's layout, we first need to retrace our steps back up to the church dedicated to *San Matteo.* The dramatic interior takes one by surprise. Baroque churches do not always make a big play of stained-glass windows. *San Matteo's* windows are set very high up and made of plain glass to allow as much light in as possible. It is the incredibly ornate stone-work that will strike you. The whole place is like a lavish art gallery. There are no pews in *San Matteo,* just simple chairs that can be stacked away to reveal the black and white, diamond-shaped tiles which form the nave. The space for the congregation is surprisingly small, dwarfed by the splendour of the rest of the church. For some reason or other, *San Matteo* is my favourite church in Lecce. That is probably why it figures in my second novel, *The Demise of Judge Grassi.* You will see the pulpit 'perched half way up to heaven' as the unusual young priest explains to his congregation. This is also where the bewildered Judge has his moment of startling revelation. Enough ecclesiastical details! From now on, I will let each church you visit impress you with its own particular mystique.

I think it would be wise of me to adopt a similar approach to the *trattorie* and other eating places in Lecce. I would advise you to be wary of the restaurants and *pizzerie* dotted up and down the two main arterial tourist streets – but even here, you won't eat badly. As a general rule, you should pop your head inside and make sure that there are plenty of Italians occupying the tables. This test does *not* apply to McDonalds, of course! What I will do is limit myself to those restaurants where I have always eaten well, letting you discover other places for yourselves. The first such restaurant is just a few steps up a narrow road immediately opposite the church of *San Matteo.* It is called *La Trattoria Nonna Tetti.* It is invisible from the church steps. But when it is open, a member of staff comes out and hangs the restaurant sign up on a pair of hooks. The address is *Piazzetta Regina Maria 17.*

At the *Nonna Tetti* you will eat good *Salentino* food for a very modest sum. The ambience is delightfully traditional, with its warm interior stone walls and arched stone ceiling. The waiters seem to be from Eastern Europe rather than Italian; sadly, this may be one the reasons why the food is relatively inexpensive. It is popular with tourists as well as Italians and retains the cosy feel of a genuine local restaurant. In the good old days, the aforementioned brightly coloured transsexual used to frequent this eating place too.

A word of warning about ALL the eating places in Salento; if you order the *antipasti della casa,* the house starters, you will have little room left for anything else. It's a difficult decision to make since the inhabitants of Salento specialise in a whole variety of tantalisingly good *antipasti.* But they do constitute a meal in themselves.

Well, I won't dwell too much on the food at this point. Leaving the *Nonna Tetti* for later if you aren't hungry yet, we should walk back up the street towards the main *Piazza.* Leading away from *La Piazza Sant'Oronzo,* is the principal pedestrian street called *Via Vittorio Emanuele,* leading straight to the spacious *Piazza del Duomo* with its lofty bell-tower. After dusk, you will be joined by amicable crowds of

Leccesi enjoying their evening *passeggiata* along this largely pedestrianized old street.

On the way up the *Via Vittorio Emanuele,* before you arrive at the *Piazza del Duomo,* you will pass other sights, including another beautiful church and, on your right, a courtyard and former monastery called *Il Palazzo dei Teatini,* where various exhibitions and gatherings are held during the course of the year. Well worth a wander round when the courtyard is open.

There is a Tourist Office on this side of the road. Strangely enough, and typical of this somewhat enigmatic part of the world, the opening times of the tourist office used to be influenced by the assumption that visitors would be so taken up with the wonders of the city that they would not feel the urge to make enquiries about it. But all this has changed over the last few years, as the local council realises that Lecce has become a popular tourist destination. New tourist offices have sprung up like mushrooms – and they stay open until late in the evening – even staying open at lunchtime. The main tourist office is now situated on the Piazza Sant-Oronzo – and the staff are engagingly helpful, served by young men and women who are anxious to show off their skills in various languages; English in particular, Our precious language may soon become our one-and-only item of export. This comment was added at the end of 2020

– after the two dreaded 'B' words became common currency. Yes, I mean Boris and Brexit!

A few steps up the street and you will come to a narrow gap between the shops and bars on your left. Suddenly, you will understand why you came to Lecce – just to see the *Piazza del Duomo.* Its sheer dimensions will take your breath away. Don't forget to visit the *Museo Diocesano* on the right flank of the *Piazza* as you are looking at the cathedral. Above all, make sure you revisit the *Piazza del Duomo* after dark, when its true magic emerges. I once took a photograph of the *Piazza* at night time and was surprised, when I later studied the photo, to see a wraith-like image hovering above the heads of the people gathered in the square. 'Must be a manifestation of The Holy Spirit,' I told myself fancifully – until I remembered that 'somebody' – possibly *me* - had been smoking a cigar at the time.

On leaving the *Piazza del Duomo,* you will see a little workshop where you can buy aprons of all shapes and sizes. The owner, Veronica, a lady in her late thirties or early forties, will sit at an antiquated, hand-operated machine while she embroiders your name and any wording you wish to put on the front of the apron – such as *Giuseppe – The best cook in Italy.* If you are stuck for ideas as to lightweight presents to take back to England, this is the place to come to! She had even taken on a teenage lad called Daniele as an apprentice – thus diminishing the number of Italy's unemployed youngsters by one.

Our main tour of orientation is nearly over. On leaving the *Piazza del Duomo,* turn left and continue to walk along the street – now called *Via G. Libertini.* This will take you past other baroque churches and various restaurants and bars as far as the beautiful *Porta Rudiae,* which is the second ancient entrance to the city. Outside the gate, everyday city life is a bustling confusion of cars, cycles, people, students and a small, permanent fruit and vegetable market. Retrace your steps as far as the cathedral square. The other arterial street, *Via Giuseppe Palmieri,* is immediately opposite the entrance to the *Piazza del Duomo.* This street will take you past a famous *pizzeria* called *Carlo V* – after the aforementioned king of the castle – and from there down to the principal historical entrance to the city – the imposing *Porta Napoli* with its pristinely sand-blasted triumphal arch. The *Teatro Paisiello* can be found just before you reach the arch. You will notice another group of fascist era buildings attached to a modern-looking glass-fronted main entrance on the north side of the arch. These form part of Lecce University's campus. It was founded in 1955 and has since been renamed *L'Università del Salento,* in the hope of giving it wider appeal. Lecce University, however, does have world-class Bio-medical and Nanotechnology sections, as well as strong Law and Economics faculties. The university buildings are dotted all around the city. The newer faculties are housed outside Lecce in modern buildings.

I believe that the presence of university students always brings fresh life to a city. The truly remarkable thing is that, come Friday afternoon, a large proportion of the students can be seen trundling their suitcases along behind them, heading for the railway station or a bus stop. Their destination - would you credit it? - they are going back home to *mamma* and the family with a case load of clothes to be washed and ironed before their return on Monday morning at the crack of dawn. It was a phenomenon that struck me in my early days as a humble English teacher at the University – in such sharp contrast to England, where students try to get a place in a university as far away as possible from their parents. And, do you know, when I talked to my students about this weekend migration, they all told me how happy they were to be going back home for a day or so, even though it often meant sharing a bedroom with younger siblings. *Vive la difference!*

If you are still not feeling the pangs of hunger, then the next paragraph can be ignored. But for those of you whose gastric juices are on the move, there are a number of excellent and interesting eating places to satisfy your taste buds in the vicinity of the *Porta Napoli.*

If you take the street which leads directly away from the arch towards the periphery of Lecce, you will be in *Via Taranto.* You can't miss it, since there is an ornate obelisk standing in the middle of the main road – sand-blasted clean just like the magnificent Triumphal Arch that marks *La Porta Napoli.* After twelve minutes' walk up this street, you will come across *La Trattoria Mamma Rita.* You will find yourself in the company of families, office workers and manual workers. It is always busy. A whole restaurant full of *Leccesi* can't be wrong. That's why it is such a good place to go and eat. It is well off the tourist track, so the prices are low and the food is always good.

The second choice is a bit more sophisticated but is less than half a kilometre's walk from *La Porta Napoli.* Go a few paces back down *Via G. Palmieri.* Just past the theatre on the left, there is a turning up a side street. You will come across our second restaurant after a brief walk, during which you will be busy dodging the cars as their drivers hurtle back home for lunch. Fortunately, it is a one-way street, so the task of remaining unharmed is a lot easier. The restaurant, on the corner of a narrow cul-de-sac, is called *Alle Due Corti.* The owner, Rosalba, and her son have built up an international reputation by specialising in preparing dishes which are typical of Salento. The *antipasti* are a culinary delight, as are the dishes that follow. The restaurant only falls down on the coffee at the end of the meal – a small price to pay. *Alle Due Corti* is well worth a visit if you want a taste of true regional cooking. Many of the restaurants claim to offer you *piatti tipici* – local dishes - but Rosalba really does it to perfection. Indeed, the menu is written in Salentino dialect, rather than in Italian, conveniently translated into English.

But for today, I would like to take you on a completely different kind of eating experience; to the kind of trattoria which we can only reminisce about in modern England, with its endless chain of Asks, Prezzos, Zizis and Stradas and the financial ruin to your wallet which follows a meal which has scant similarity to anything truly Italian. When you emerge from the *Osteria Da Angiulino,* you will wonder why on earth you ever bother to eat out in England. Little gems like *Da Angiulino* can be found all over Italy if you can only winkle them out. After lunch, we shall already be well placed to complete our preliminary tour of the city of Lecce.

Take the street which leads away from *Porta Napoli,* at right angles to *Via G. Palmieri.* It is called *Via Principe di Savoia.* You will have to be careful not to walk right past the *Osteria Da Angiulino* without noticing it. Walking along *Via*

Principe di Savoia, you will pass a piazza on your left, set back from the road. Our *trattoria* is a little bit further down the street on your left. The restaurant name is carved modestly into the stonework of the building. You will be struck by the simplicity of the furnishings and the seemingly deliberate informality of the place. If you are greeted by an unsmiling young man who gives you a hard, disconcerting stare, as if you are an intruder invading the privacy of his home, then you have met Angiulino's son. He has taken over the running of the joint from his ageing father. Don't worry about the stare; he does it quite knowingly in order to test your resolve at having chosen *his* eating place out of all the others in Lecce. He has an underlying mischievous sense of humour and probably a heart of gold. However, I have to say that the last time we presented ourselves there we were turned away because we hadn't booked a table. The power of the internet is to blame, I would imagine.

The food is simple and excellent, originally cooked quite literally 'just as granny used to cook it'. They do a brilliant *Parmigiana di Melanzane* and a tasty *Fave e Cicoria* as a *primo piatto.* The first dish is, as you probably know, cooked aubergines, tomato sauce and mozzarella. The second dish, which you can find on every menu in the region, is a wholesome combination of mashed broad beans, potatoes and Parmesan cheese served with chicory. It is laced with olive oil and eaten with pieces of toasted bread. A *'must'* at some stage of your visit!

The rest of the menu is simple and excellent – including a delicious *pezzeti di cavallo al sugo* - a piquant horse meat stew. In the years that I went there, the menu never changed once. The place is always full at lunchtime and in the evenings too, with a goodly mixture of locals and Italian tourists too. As in *all* eating places in Italy, you can order a carafe of wine, from a quarter litre to one litre. You will get simple, drinkable wine for just a few euros. None of this wine by the glass nonsense that we have to put up with in England, which will cost you *un'occhio della testa!* *(An eye of the head, or an arm and a leg as I mentioned before.)*

After lunch, and an injunction from Angiulino's son that you have to return the following day on penalty of being excommunicated, we shall turn left out of the restaurant and follow the street until we reach *Via Umberto 1,* which is a right turn into a broad and beautiful street leading past the municipal *palazzo* and right up to the most magnificent façade in the whole of Lecce. This is the church called *La Santa Croce.* While you stroll up this piazza-like street, take a look through the big double wooden doors that lead into the magnificent garden courtyards, where a handful of fortunate *Leccesi* have their apartments. Such garden courtyards are dotted round Lecce at strategic points. But more about that in a minute.

You can hardly spend less than a quarter of an hour admiring the façade of *La Santa Croce* in disbelief whilst attempting to capture the whole effect in one Smartphone photograph. It is unbelievably ornate. If you look inside the church, you might find mass going on. The ornate baroque carvings will continue to defy reality. It is impossible to visit this church and not come out with your atheistic tendencies shaken to the core. Our forebears' belief in God must have been unshakable to have gone to the lengths involved in creating this place of worship some five hundred years ago.

A short distance on foot, and you are back in the *Piazza Sant'Oronzo* where we started out. After a coffee in one of the indoor or outdoor bars, you can explore the rest of the city at leisure. Or have your *pennichella* – a nap – after overestimating the amount of food you ordered *da Angiulino.* As I am leaving you to your own devices, I would whole-heartedly recommend that you wander round the maze of little streets behind the *Duomo.* You will come unexpectedly across a host of picturesque *piazze* and pretty courtyards, where the real *Leccesi* live out their lives. You should be rewarded by the sight of an old gnarled olive tree that has wrapped itself into the fabric of the building. Take a photo – otherwise the folk at home just won't believe you!

I have talked at great length about Lecce. It is inevitable, I'm afraid. It is the most beautiful city in Puglia – by a long shot. To do Lecce real justice, you have to live there from day to day until the city becomes part of your soul; or until you are absorbed into its fabric. I will content myself with giving you a few more hints as to the rest of the city before we head further south to visit the rest of *Salento.*

For starters, there are many eating places that deserve your attention. I want to mention a pizzeria called *La Perla*, which is not far from the *Castello Carlo V.* Ask anyone for directions there – it is a much-loved destination for pizza lovers. At *La Perla,* you can eat pizzas cooked in a traditional wood-burning oven for just four euros; the most expensive pizzas on the menu cost a mere €6.50 – such a far cry from Pizza Express and Dominos in this country. *La Perla* has a complete non-pizza menu too. Even a bottle of excellent *Primitivo di Manduria* only costs €10. The house wine might just rack the price of your meal up by two euros.

There is also a well-known *Slow Food* restaurant – they really do use this term untranslated – called *L'Osteria degli Spiriti.* It is near the public gardens. It is always full because it is small. It is run by an owner who promotes local cuisine in a traditional ambience. How wonderful to find a place to eat which is the exact opposite in every respect to the aforementioned American culinary disaster. However, I must stress again that there will certainly be other excellent restaurants and *trattorie* that I simply have not been to.

There is a modern part of Lecce too – where all the fashionable shops and a smattering of supermarkets are. Just walk past the ice-cream and cake shop *Natale,* cross over the road at the lights and keep walking in a straight line down *Via Trinchese* for about a kilometre. You will arrive in a wide, modern piazza with fountains in the middle surrounded by shady trees and endless numbers of parked cars. This is where Lecce's normal, commercial life takes place. The square is surrounded by shops and spacious flats. It's all quite tasteful in a modern kind of way.

If you happen to be in Lecce over a weekend at the end of May or beginning of June, it is worth while checking up whether your visit coincides with a splendid annual event called *Cortili Aperti* – Open Courtyards. This civic event was begun way back in 1995. Another secret of this amazing city is revealed. Behind the façade of the historic centre, concealed by massive wooden doors lie Lecce's hidden gardens and courtyards. Little wooden doors inserted into the main doors allow the fortunate inhabitants to enter or leave without revealing their secret lives to the rest of the world. The big wooden doors are flung open once a year. It is like a magic trick; walking down Lecce's narrow streets on normal days, you can have no notion that such gardens and courtyards exist. It is a startling phenomenon – little enclaves of peace and quiet within the heart of the city are suddenly revealed, adding a whole new dimension of space and time to this unique place. Each courtyard and garden will be occupied by singers and musicians – often students from the University's Music Department – all contributing their particular talents to this extraordinary event. When I went there one year, there was a grand piano in one of the courtyards being played expertly by a classical pianist; a student who might have been twenty-one years old. There is a feeling of culture about the whole event that it is rare to find in England. However, it has to be said, the event is extremely popular nowadays. You are one of a horde of spectators milling around the narrow streets until late at night.

'All of Lecce is a stage'.

So, finally, what can I say about the actors on this stage? They are a motley crew as you might expect. They certainly debunk the preconception prevalent amongst their northern cousins that southern Italians are lazy, crafty and somewhat lacking in intelligence – a general drag on the Italian economy, in fact. Southern Italians are ruled by one over-riding factor: their immediate family - which may well include every aunt, uncle, cousin, parent or grandparent – will always take priority. As you piece the puzzle together, you realise that your new acquaintances do not, in general, have to travel very far to be reunited with their kith and kin. I don't know how it is with you, in England, but my family is spread around the globe. It is at once a comfort yet an inescapable commitment to have ones extended family living on the doorstep.

In Lecce, I got to know some educated, cultured, hard-working and highly intelligent people – including a scientist who understood nanotechnology as if it was a recipe for pasta with tomato sauce. I taught English to a pair of beautiful twin girls who waltzed into the top universities in Rome through sheer intellectual ability. I have witnessed men repairing or building houses from six o'clock in the morning to get as much work done as possible before the sun made life too hot to work. Musicians seem to sprout up from every corner of the city. A brass band can be conjured up out of thin air to play on piazzas or to escort the lately departed souls to the nearest cemetery. Even the humblest individuals seem to exude a kind of confidence that says *'I've got a right to be here, you know!'* to those around them. The one thing that struck me above all else, in the early days, was that southern Italians smile a lot less than we do, and they don't say 'sorry' for every silly little peccadillo. They are, quite rightly, more sparing with their laughter and their apologies.

Have you ever been to a pub or restaurant in England where alcohol-swilling punters are laughing uproariously and deafeningly every few minutes at some inane comment by a member of their company? In this part of the world, maybe in Italy as a whole, the main sound in a bar or restaurant is the agreeable resonance of people talking to each other and sometimes sharing a humorous moment together.

I do not wish to paint the picture of a utopian world. That, too, would be far from the truth. Unemployment, drugs and the mafia are ever present – even if beneath the surface. In my early days, I was appalled to see couples careering around on Vespa scooters in Lecce's busy streets with an un-helmeted child wedged between them. Even nowadays, it is common to see people driving around in cars without seat-belts attached – their argument being: 'But I'm only going shopping!' or 'My home is only five minutes away'.

Yes, they can be very irritating. But above all else, they are acutely aware that their lives are to be *lived* during every waking moment. These actors on life's stage do not have the luxury of understudies, or people prompting them from the wings. They realise that every moment spent strutting or fretting upon the stage of life counts in the greater scheme of things. They are past masters at making up the script as they go.

When I was in Lecce in November 2014, I heard a distressing account of a new café owner whose front doors had been torched overnight. An ex-colleague of mine overheard the owner, a woman, talking tearfully to a customer the following day.

"I'm not going to give into them," she was saying, "whatever they do to me!"

Obviously, she had not paid her *pizzo* to the local mob – and courageously had no intention of doing so.

To offset the grim reality of Puglia's sinister undercurrents, a colleague told me about a local grocery shop owned by two brothers. I used to shop there for cheese and *salami* myself. One brother works there religiously every day. His sibling habitually strutted self-importantly round the shop looking superior, but contributing nothing to the running of the establishment. It is rumoured that, when not doing his strutting act in the shop, he likes to stand high up above the street on his balcony, in full view of passers-by, wearing nothing at all under his dressing gown. I understand from a more recent conversation with my friend and colleague that this gentleman has taken to walking along the side streets dressed as a woman.

All the city's a stage...

3:   *O Salento mio! Gallipoli...*

(Going south out of Lecce down the Ionian coast)

It isn't *my* Salento, I regret to say. It's *theirs,* of course. People whom I got to know would constantly ask: *'Ma conosci veramente il nostro bellissimo Salento, Reach Hard?'*

('Do you really know how beautiful our Salento is, Richard?')

I got used their attractive, if vaguely improper, mispronunciation of my first name - rolling the 'r's' and emphasising the aspirate 'h'. Some didn't bother attempting the English pronunciation, so I got called *Riccardo,* which I infinitely prefer to 'Richard' anyway. Just think of all the Richards you've ever come across and tell me if any one of them is remotely 'normal'. More often than not, they addressed me as *professore.* Their obsession with addressing everybody by their title is a deep-rooted social convention, which I singularly failed to shake with my Anglo-Saxon over-familiarity.

'Oh yes! I know your beautiful Salento alright. It is burnt into my very soul.'

It was not a question of love at first sight, however. Salento is basically flat with a few modest hills to which they optimistically attach the epithet *'monte'.* It is, incidentally one of the very few areas of Italy that is not prone to earthquakes – nor even occasional tremors.

Olive trees, set in silvery green olive groves, outnumber all other types of tree by about ten million to one. The vast majority of these 'ancient' olive groves were planted in the 1950s. Mussolini began the regeneration of southern Italy during his reign. What with his railway building and road building schemes, he managed to do a great deal for Puglia until, like so many dictators before and since, he became obsessed with a desire to rule the world, as his vast ego expanded to bursting point. Do we see evidence of the same phenomenon here in the UK today?

I was once told by a man called Claudio, pointing at an olive tree in his garden, that this was "a *secolare* tree". "I thought it was an olive tree," I ventured. "It IS", he replied. Claudio was hoping that the word for 'centuries old' would be the same word in English. The said tree was indeed gnarled and twisted like a venerable old man. One of the thousands of olive trees which existed before Mussolini's expansion plan.

Puglia arguably produces the best olive oil anywhere in the world – not to mention some of the best wines too. But, on this latter point, I might be prejudiced. You will have to decide for yourselves. I shall talk about Puglia's wines at a later stage – the many excellent Puglian wines do not come exclusively from Salento.

Only the coastline can honestly be described as 'spectacular' - and not all of it automatically deserves that epithet. But it certainly has more than its fair share of breath-defying vistas. You might come across a seaside resort called Mancaversa. Claudio, the school secretary's fiancé where I first taught, kindly took me to this seaside resort in the early days. This is the same Claudio who showed me the *secolare* tree, by the way. He wanted to impress me as to Salento's most attractive aspects. On the beach, I observed a dumped refrigerator and other items of household detritus.

'Washed up by the sea,' he explained dismissively. 'The cruise ships dump their rubbish overboard and it gets washed up.'

Apart from the unlikelihood of jettisoning a whole refrigerator overboard, I forbore to point out to Claudio that the Ionian Sea is virtually tide-less and that, in any case, the fridge was well above the tide line. He was evidently in a state of denial about his *'Bel Salento.'* I am certain I must be mistaken about this seaside resort. Hundreds of *Salentini* – and Germans - swear by it. It must have just been a bad Mancaversa day – and it *was* very much out of season.

But despite the grievances, Salento's charms creep up on you over time – like a secret lover who stealthily slips into your bed in the small hours of the morning. To this day, I am not quite sure how the indigenous spirits succeeded in bringing about my total seduction. Maybe I shall discover the key to it all as this narrative unfolds. Or perhaps it was simply because I happened to be in love with a particularly beautiful *Salentina* at the time. (That's a woman from these parts, in case you were wondering.)

Down to business! We are now going on a glorious journey of discovery south of Lecce. I assume you will have rented a car. If not, then you could rent one from several car hire companies in Lecce. Your other alternative requires a bit more courage and a sense of adventure and involves taking the local trains, which depart regularly from Lecce station. They are run by a separate company to the mainline trains which go up north. The intercity trains 'terminate' at Lecce and simply do not venture into rural Salento by even one metre.

You would find yourself travelling on the *Ferrovie Sud-Est (South-Eastern-Railways)*. I promise you that the experience is worth your while – even if you fight shy of ever repeating the venture. First of all, you have to find the ticket office, which is situated half way up the main platform. The line divides into two distinct routes, so you need to decide on your destination. It is quite feasible to take a train down to Gallipoli for the day. The platforms dedicated to the *FSE* are on the far side of the station. Here confusion reigns for the uninitiated traveller. Station staff or other passengers are always willing to reassure you that you are on the right train. Depending on the time of day, there are substantial numbers of secondary school students going to or from Lecce back to their towns and villages. Don't worry, they are amazingly civilised compared to their English counterparts. It's all to do with the fact that family life in general still holds sway. There will also be university students on their daily commute into or out of Lecce. The rest of the population tend to take coaches – a *Pullman* - or, more likely, opt to travel by car.

It is rare for each train to be more than two carriages long. The rolling stock used to be from the WW2 era. I understand that the trains used to be in service in the prosperous north of Italy until they grew too old and noisy for their liking. So they were shunted down to Puglia where they could live out the remainder of their days in the service of the 'poor relations' down south. New rolling stock is slowly replacing the old trains, I have been reliably informed. But last time I travelled by the *Sud-Est* nothing seemed to have altered all that much – apart from the fact that the level crossing barriers had become electrically operated. Even in the early 21st century, it was the FSE staff, at each individual station who had to wind the barriers down laboriously via a crank handle and lengths of heavy cabling running along the tracks.

But, unbelievably, there is a guard on every single train – as well as a driver, of course. Not only that, but each little station has a uniformed station-master to usher passengers on and off the train. Tall palm trees rustle in the breeze and the station masters take an obvious pride in the state of their stations. The FSE organises an annual competition to see whose station is the smartest and has the best-kept flower displays. It feels more like travelling used to be on branch lines in England in the mid twentieth century when I was a youngster. The station master is there to shout 'Via' to the train driver to send the ancient, grumbling diesel train on its way – or even one of the new trains if you are unlucky!

This very non-technical manner of shouting 'Via' – 'on your way' – can backfire. I once witnessed a schoolboy of about fifteen, who shouted out 'Via' as he got off the train. A sleepy driver began to pull out of the station as if on automatic pilot while passengers were still getting on and off the train. I had the impression that the stationmaster had cuffed the delinquent round the ears – judging by the language that issued from the chastised boy's lips. Long live the old-fashioned ways!

The old trains rumble and sway along the single track past little farm buildings and through countless olive groves and vineyards. This is unchanged Salento as it has been for centuries. You are on a time-warp journey through an ancient land. The experience is well worth the trouble, despite the inevitable delays of travelling on a single track railway system. One minor delay along the track and the whole system is thrown *'in tilt'*. I've no idea how Italians invented this English-sounding phrase to signify a technical breakdown. I could not persuade them that it was not an expression in common use in current English.

'Why haven't you done your homework?" I would ask my students.

'Sorry, *professore* - my computer is in tilt.'

I was too busy telling them that the phrase is not real English, or supplying them with a more viable linguistic excuse, to remonstrate with them for having failed to produce their homework.

On your way down to Gallipoli, you will pass through 'my' village, Sannicola. The guard-cum-ticket-inspector will know whether anyone is getting off at these minor stations and instruct the driver accordingly. If there is even one solitary passenger on the platform the driver will bring the train to a brake-grinding halt.

My journeys were all so spontaneous, quirky and haphazard on the *Ferrovie Sud-Est.* I shall never forget them. On one of my early trips into Lecce, I had been warned by my colleague, Glynis, about the vagaries of the system.

'Do I have to change trains?' I asked the ticket inspector.

'We don't know yet,' he replied in all seriousness. 'I'll tell you when we reach...' I couldn't catch the name of the station.

So, at least one trip on the *FSE,* is really worth the trouble in order to experience a world that is simply not our world. I loved it – until I got myself a yellow Fiat Panda to get me around. The sheer convenience and versatility of a car was irresistible.

Tragically, after decades of travelling in this way – along single line tracks – there occurred in 2016 a collision on the FSE – killing a number of passengers. The accident happened well to the north of Lecce. An investigation is still going on as I write these words. Human error, I fear, will be the outcome of investigations. A tragedy indeed if this sad accident spells the end of an era for life as it used to be lived.

As you rattle – safely - through the landscape down south towards Gallipoli, take a look at the rich red colour of the iron-laden soil. Salento has been described, by a well-known local wine producer *(Mottura)* as a tongue of earth flanked by the Ionian and the Adriatic seas. At its most basic, that is quite a fair description of Salento; it can grow things in great profusion; exotic things like vines, olive trees and such a cornucopia of fruit and vegetables as to make it impossible for you not to eat healthily.

I suppose that, as you've managed to brave the train journey down to Gallipoli, we may as well start with this unusual town. It is well worth spending time and photo-space on your iPhones in this lively settlement – with its own dialect, its own *carnevale,* which takes place colourfully every February - and its very own mafia clan, too.

The name of the town is derived from the Greek *Kali + Polis,* meaning beautiful city. Gallipoli has just over 20 000 inhabitants, which is a nice comfortable size for a town. Traditionally, it lived off its fishing industry. Now stocks have diminished to such an extent that it can no longer entirely support the town's economy. Gallipoli is a popular tourist attraction during the latter part of July and all of August.

During the holiday season, it is difficult to find a spot on the beaches on which to park your towel; even worse, trying to find a place to park your car. But a visit to Gallipoli out of season is an experience not to be forgotten. Best to check the return train times to Lecce before you wander off into the town; there is an almost total lack of trains going back up the line before late afternoon – when the kids come out of school.

The kids, as I have already said, will not be disruptive – even if they all talk at once with the volume turned up to loud. This is a necessity throughout the whole of Italy – even on TV political debates – to ensure that your personal viewpoint is heard. The astounding thing is that they all seem to be able to understand what the others are saying and can argue their case quite logically, whereas to us, it just sounds like a cacophony of voices.

Talking of 'uncouth behaviour', I recently read an article in one of our national newspapers about the "unacceptable" behaviour of certain tourists in Gallipoli, who had been upsetting the locals by their 'lewd antics' on the beaches. The word 'dogging' has been adopted by the Italians with no attempt to translate the word into their own language. What a very pagan pastime for such a devoutly Catholic part of the world! It is all part of the *degrado* of young people's morals, it seems. A difficult one for the locals since they – and the local mafia - depend increasingly on the money brought in by tourists. I am sure it is only a minority of tourists and, at least, it is restricted to the month of August, when anyone local with any sense at all will go on holiday somewhere else – or just stay at home and grin and bear the temporary invasion. The moral of this digression is: visit Salento in the period between September and the early part of July. That gives you plenty of scope and you will see it at its best. Now, back to the everyday face of Gallipoli...

The trains 'terminate' at Gallipoli so there is little problem about choosing which train to take you back up north to Lecce. But you need to ask because there is a train that goes off cross country to Casarano. Even so, you would be able to pick up a train to Lecce from there if you needed to.

Have you noticed how trains in England always 'terminate' these days as soon as they arrive at their destination? In the case of the *FSE* rolling stock, you may well wonder how long the older locomotives will go on before some vital part shakes itself to bits – and 'terminates' in the proper sense of the word.

Gallipoli station itself backs on to the port, which is full of fishing boats plus a stray, gun metal grey battleship belonging to the Italian navy. You will walk up a gentle incline along a pleasant avenue lined with tall palm trees to reach the main road that runs through the modern part of the town, lined with ice cream parlours, pizzerias, clothes shops and dozens of jewellers' shops. On the corner of this short avenue, you will pass a restaurant called *'Da Olga'*. It's a good place to eat but not the best setting if you want a view over the sea. This was the first restaurant where I ate a plate of pasta with mussels and cannellini beans mixed in with a light tomato sauce - a delicious combination, by the way, and a speciality of Gallipoli.

Turn right and walk towards Gallipoli's *centro storico* less than a kilometre away. You will be glad you came by train when you see how few parking spaces there are left along the main road. All the side streets have cars piled up in amiable disorder too.

But Gallipoli is full of Mediterranean light and the smell of fish and the sea. Please try to ignore, on your walk along the wide and pleasant avenue, a monstrosity of the sixties or seventies which rises up several stories high. Its glass and concrete structure is an eyesore and an insult to a nation that ought to know better. But that was the seventies for you! The rest of the town is a delight. You will quickly reach the 'causeway' that divides the new town from the original *centro storico* that you are heading towards. Just before you cross the causeway leading to Old Gallipoli, you will come across the ancient *Fontana Greca (The Greek Fountain)* on your left. The Greek influence is very present in this ancient town. The fountain is a beautiful monument to Gallipoli's past with its ornate yet weather-beaten carvings.

Look along the quayside beyond the *Fontana Greca*. Right at the end of the promenade, you will see a quaint little church called *La Chiesa di Santa Maria del Cannetto*. If it is open, go and have a peek inside. It is, I was told, every local girl's dream to be married in this church. To your right of the causeway, you should see a 'floating' restaurant – where I have never eaten, having been warned about the prices they charge. But prices in this part of the world generally seem cheap compared to eating out in the UK. But bear in mind, too, that the more you pay for a meal down here, the more you may be helping to swell the coffers of the local mafia clan. A sobering thought – and one that is best ignored. By doing so, you will be at one with the majority of the population here, who have to turn a blind eye to the inconspicuous reality behind the magnificent façades.

Never mind about food - or the underworld - for the time being. Gallipoli is open to the sea on all sides. It is full of swooping gulls and boats rocking gently on the waters. And the whole atmosphere is redolent of seaweed, fish and ozone. The *Salentino* coastline stretches invitingly to the north and the south as far as the eye can see, seducing you with its magnetic pull in both directions simultaneously.

As you walk up towards the old town, glancing to your left, you will notice a giant replica of a sea-urchin sticking out of the water. I can never quite decide whether this adds to or detracts from the appeal of the town. Certainly when it is compared to the glass and concrete monstrosity you have just passed in the new town, this sea-urchin is a work of art.

Soon you will reach the old part of the town. Nothing that you have seen so far can prepare you for the experience that awaits you. You have two immediate dilemmas to resolve, however; should you turn left or right to go anticlockwise or clockwise round the *centro storico?* Or should you dive into the labyrinth of narrow streets that constitute the almost perfectly preserved old town? I am pleased to say that it does not really matter either way – so long as you find time to do both. Whatever route you take, you will be doubly delighted at not having to find a parking place for a car. If you *do* come by car to Gallipoli, please leave it parked near the port in the new part of the town. Only the locals seem to know where this parking zone is situated. Parking here used to be free. Recently, I noticed, parking metres have been installed – but there are always spaces available. Attempting to drive into the old part of the town would be a decision you would deeply regret. Indeed, during the summer months, a hidden camera will take a picture of your number plate and you will receive a hefty fine – whether you manage to find a parking space or not.

Let's turn left and walk round the periphery of the old town in a clockwise direction, which gives you a dazzling panorama of the harbour and the sea below. Unless you are a lone traveller, you will be forced to walk single file for some of the stroll. If ever there was a place in the world which was *not* intended for the motor car, it is old Gallipoli. At best, the pedestrian sidewalk is narrow, but there are various vantage points where you can safely stand and admire the sandy beach below the city wall. The beach can easily be accessed from above. You might get the impression that the cars, either parked or struggling to negotiate the narrow strip of tarmac, outnumber the human beings by ten to one. The trouble, as you will discover later, is that the streets inside the old town are simply too narrow to park a vehicle. Thus, car owners are forced to park along the peripheral street.

On a fine day, when the turquoise waters are calm, you can see rocks just below the surface of the Ionian Sea that seem to shift with the current like huge black fish. A white lighthouse, some distance away, stands guard over the coastline. I love this breath-taking view in all weathers – and in all seasons.

If any of the little churches that line the route are open, then dive inside them while you can. Their modest facades hide unexpected baroque treasures inside that can be seen in no other part of the world. And they are all so diverse. I was convinced that one of them was the seat of Satan rather than the Holy Spirit. It looked and felt sinister - there is no other word for it. We were approached by the doyen of the place, who told us weird and wonderful tales of the Black Virgin of somewhere or other, before ushering us out into the real world again. Maybe it was simply his lunchtime and he wanted to lock up. I cannot remember the church's name and have not been able to find it again since the first and only visit. But Gallipoli is like that – it is the keeper of a myriad little mysteries and unexpected secrets.

As you walk round to the other side of the old town – the distance is really very short – the coastline stretches invitingly up north, winding round a long, sandy beach and a rocky coastline, which disappears into the blue hazy distance. A massive watchtower stands sentinel over the Ionian Sea at the limits of your vision. We shall head up the coast afterwards.

You will pass a number of inviting restaurants with panoramic views stretching to the horizon. You will probably eat well in any of them. Those that fail to satisfy hungry Italian stomachs would simply not survive. Beware of ordering freshly caught fish which are priced by the kilo on the menus. Some of the restaurateurs might just take advantage of your foreignness to overcharge you. I found this out to my cost in the early days when I had a meal without my Italian companion present to protect me from the wiles of her fellow-countrymen. Judging by the price I paid for that fish, it should have been the size of a small whale.

You will eventually arrive back where you started. How long 'eventually' lasts will depend on the number of churches you have visited or the amount of time you have spent taking in the seascape. Just before the circle is complete, you will come across a restaurant called *Il Pescatore – The Fisherman.* It is a good, straightforward place to enjoy seafood and is favoured by locals. There are similarly good eating places inside the walls too – if perchance you are lucky enough to find yourself in the right part of the labyrinth inside the old town.

Start off on the second leg of your walk round Gallipoli as if you were going to walk round the outside again. This time, however, take the first main turning to the right that takes you past the tourist shops, ice cream parlours and all the other purveyors of goods essential to the traveller. You will even come across mini-supermarkets and normal shops where the natives go to acquire the necessities of life.

Even if you don't believe in God Almighty or the Pope, you just have to go and wonder at the newly restored

Duomo, which you will come across immediately after the shops. The cathedral sits on the highest point of the circular peninsula. It is baroque down to its cornerstone. It is dedicated to *Santa Agata* – Virgin and Martyr. The inside has been restored to all its former glory. The cathedral is officially designated a national treasure and matches – or even surpasses – many of the churches you have visited in Lecce. You will quickly appreciate why. The paintings are nothing short of breath-taking. The elaborately carved wooden pulpit is perched half way up to heaven in the nave. Should you ever read my second novel, *The Demise of Judge Grassi,* you might be interested to know that this church was my inspiration for the unforgettable sermons and the priest who delivered them - although the 'action' was transferred to *San Matteo* in Lecce. The text for his sermon was from the Gospel of Saint Matthew where it says: 'The last shall be first and the first last'. I had never witnessed a sermon before where the children were actively participating in the event – alternately standing and sitting at the priest's instructions. "Those of you who think you're important, STAND UP" he said invitingly. All the children who stood up were then asked to sit down at the same moment as the timid ones rose hesitatingly to their feet. The message was clear to all and sundry – and everybody was smiling. That's what I call a sermon!

After this amazing ecclesiastical experience, you should wander round the maze of narrow streets where real people live out their daily lives, dodging in and out of the tiny courtyards where the *mammas* hang their washing out to dry from their cramped balconies. This is the genuine article – the reason why you came to visit this unexpected place, steeped in its own past. You might be relieved to know that you won't be dodging cars – the roads are too narrow for this scourge of the modern era. Instead, the dodging will be done by youngsters riding their Vespa scooters, weaving their way round all the obstacles in their path – including you.

Look out for hidden restaurants on unexpected corners. Make sure the one where you finally choose to eat is frequented by Italians and *Gallipolini*. If in doubt, ask a local – although there is a risk that the eating-place they recommend will be run by one of their relatives. The people of Gallipoli are a very close-knit community where brothers, uncles and aunts, cousins, nephews and nieces abound.

If your stomach is susceptible to sea food, then take care in your choice of restaurant. A recent police raid by the *Guardia Costiere – the Coastal Police* - resulted in the confiscation of a load of mussels considered unfit for human consumption from a number of restaurants in Gallipoli – including a Chinese one. The owners were fined €3500 each.

It is reassuring to know that the authorities are on the lookout for such occasional transgressions. I am quite sure that neither *Il Pescatore* nor *Da Olga* was involved. Another restaurant which has an abidingly good reputation is called *La Scogliera (The Clifftop).* But I must repeat – you are unlikely to be disappointed wherever you go to eat, in this part of the world; the competition is just too fierce.

4:   O Salento Mio! *Part two – Santa Maria al Bagno...*

(Heading northwards along the coast from Gallipoli to Porto Selvaggio)

For the time being, I shall assume that you *do* have a car. The only alternative is to hire bicycles and only the Belgians are mad enough to go in for serious cycling down here in Salento. I know this to be true – I've met some of them. Really fanatically keen they can be! They would even have you believe they cycled down all the way from Belgium via France, if they thought you were that gullible. But I think it is just a tall story to explain why they are always glowing with perspiration when they dismount from their steeds, which subsequently justifies to the world why they swill down jug loads of *Peroni* whenever they stop for a break.

If you arrived in Gallipoli by car, then you have a very easy drive up the coastal road towards Santa Maria al Bagno and beyond. If you are driving down from Lecce, take the *Superstrada SS101* out of Lecce heading for Gallipoli, but come off the *superstrada* at Sannicola and head for the coast at Lido Conchiglie – this will get you to your destination much sooner. A *superstrada,* I should explain, is a highway that has not quite made it to *autostrada* status. That is to say, Italian drivers can let rip at 140 kilometres an hour rather

73

than 190 kilometres an hour as they would on a real motorway. The speed limit on a *superstrada* is, in point of fact, between 90 and 110 k.p.h.

Just be careful when you share this type of road with Italians. Remember that, when they come off the slip road in order to join the main highway, they inevitably do so without looking to see if there is anything coming up on the inside lane. I cannot suggest a reason for their bad driving habits. I still believe that such manoeuvres are carried out as a kind of act of faith on their part - nuns and priests, and the elderly are often the most perilous. Young male drivers like to show off. Be vigilant and you stand a reasonable chance of survival. I drove for nine years down here without having a single accident. But there were a few nasty, near misses. On one occasion, I have to admit, my new yellow Panda was hit by a flying plastic chair in my village, Sannicola. It had come off one those three-wheeler contraptions, called an *APE,* thrown off by the centrifugal force of the vehicle coming round a narrow bend at speed. The driver was very contrite – fearful that I would report him to the police. He was too old to have bothered with anything as new-fangled as a driving licence or insurance documents. He was no doubt driving well before the invention of driving tests. If he had ever taken a test, he would have inserted a wad of *lire* banknotes between the papers he presented - far more persuasive than any skills he might have possessed as a driver.

Back to my road directions! Before you reach Sannicola proper, you take the coastal road going off to your right towards Lido Conchiglie. You will drive over a level crossing. If you are lucky, the barrier will be down so you will have the additional pleasure of waiting for one of the *FSE* trains to rumble past on its way to or from Gallipoli. You will pass under the *superstrada* which you have just left. By then, you will already have spotted the Ionian Sea, bathed in a translucent glow as far as the distant horizon, as you descend the hill towards the coast. Cast your eye to the right and you will see a little deserted chapel on the hill top. It is worth the time and trouble to get out of your car and walk up the wild flower-scented path to this ancient building, haunted by centuries old spirits – and the odd owl. If nothing else, you have an unrestricted view of the coast below you. Whatever you decide to do, you need to turn right on to the coastal road and head for Lido Conchiglie – which is a *frazione* of Sannicola. A *frazione* – meaning a 'fraction' – is literally a split off section of the main town or village; a hamlet, according to my dictionary. If you turn left, you would be heading back down to Gallipoli.

In Salento, the local authorities have recently been spending European money installing roundabouts. Since my last visit, a couple of years previously, they have sprung up like mushrooms all over Salento. You will come across such a roundabout just a few hundred metres along the road before you reach Lido Conchiglie. LC is not a particularly attractive seaside resort – but it gives you access to the sandy beach which stretches all the way back to Gallipoli.

If, at the roundabout, you turn left off the 'main' road, you will be heading for the aforementioned beach. This is the place to go if you've got kids or if you want to swim safely in the shallow waters of the Ionian Sea. In the summer season, from mid-June until early September, this road will take you to the official parking sites, where you will have to pay to park your car and gain access to the stretch of sand for which they have responsibility.

This may seem like exploitation of a public amenity to our democratic Anglo-Saxon minds. In point of fact, the system works more in your favour than against. You have a safe place to park your car under the shade of the trees that run all along the coast here. You can buy snacks and drinks. You have toilets which are kept clean. The owners also have a responsibility to keep the beach clean and litter-free. You can bring your picnic to eat under the pine trees, or hire umbrellas and sun-loungers to shelter from the heat of the sun up above. They even have manned lookout posts to see that nobody gets into trouble while swimming. They have to fly a red flag if the waters are deemed to be unsafe for bathing. On the down side, they seem to consider it necessary to play music all the time via loud-speakers. The notion of silence seems to make Italians very anxious – *nervoso*, is their word for it. But this intrusion on the senses only happens during the high season – August.

Interestingly, all over Italy, it is the case that a narrow strip of sand between the shore line and the controlled part of the beach must, by law, remain in the free public domain. So you are legally entitled to dangle your toes in the water without paying a single *centesimo*.

The sites are usually very well managed. We always head for the one called *Le Bandiere* – owned and run by two amicable brothers called Rosario and Dario. Their out-of-season job is the manufacturing of dental equipment. They hail from nearby Sannicola. As the name *Le Bandiere* implies, it has the flags of every nation likely to visit the area hanging outside the entrance to the site, so you cannot miss it. It's in the middle of the long beach so you will have to drive a few hundred metres before you find it. The owners are *simpatici* – friendly, that is - and will greet you like old friends after a few visits. On one occasion, shoals of little fish like whitebait were spotted by the site owners. Rosario and Dario netted thousands of them, grilled them over a fire and distributed the fishes – sprinkled with salt and lemon juice - free to their clients on the beach.

In June, early July and in September, only the local population will frequent this stretch of the coast. In the high season, it can be a bit difficult to find any privacy. But "pryvacy", pronounced the American way, is an alien concept to Italians; the proof of this is that they use the English word for it, because it does not exist in Italian. They do genuinely seem to feel more secure when surrounded by hordes of their fellow countrymen. I have often chosen a deserted early morning spot on the beach all to myself. Sure enough, Italians who arrive a bit later will usually come and plonk their towels and kids as near to you as possible. It's quite reassuring in one way – you feel part of a vibrant and gregarious species of beings. The serried ranks of colourful umbrellas do not appear until the high season is underway.

If you are travelling out of season, none of these beach car parks are open. You are free to park your car anywhere along the new roads and reach the beach via any access point. Alternatively, you can park your car in Lido Conchiglie and walk south along the deserted strand back towards distant Gallipoli. It's an exhilarating experience in any season. You won't get cut off by the tide – because, as you remember, there isn't one.

The coastline above Lido Conchiglie changes dramatically. The long stretch of sand becomes rocky, with countless little inlets where, out of season, fishermen stand patiently on the rocks with their lines cast out to sea, undisturbed by the passing of the years. Many of them look as if they have survived two world wars unperturbed by such transitory events. We are now heading for Santa Maria al Bagno along a road that hugs the coast. To make this journey possible, a large chunk of the cliff has been dynamited away in order to build the road. The locals optimistically call this section of the coast *Il Monte Spaccato* – the Cleft Mountain. In fairly flat Puglia, I suppose, retrospectively, it must have seemed like a mountain before it was blown apart by a couple of sticks of dynamite. Talking of explosives, some of the less scrupulous locals were not past using a stick of explosive to dislodge colonies of mussels stuck to rocks beneath the surface. They can, in this illegal manner, reap a much more abundant harvest than those who patiently pick them off the rocks one by one. I learnt this piece of local news when I first arrived in Salento. It may well be that the practice has been outlawed nowadays – it was never legal anyway.

After following the beautiful rocky coastline for a kilometre or so, you will pass *Le Quattro Colonne* on your left. Four ancient stone towers rising out of the ground give this place its name. This magnificent edifice is what remains of a castle built by *Carlo V* to defend his land against the Saracens – *et al.* The building seems to be a restaurant nowadays. It was a discotheque. It might still become one when darkness falls.

We soon arrive at the enchanting little resort of Santa Maria al Bagno. *Il bagno* – the bathroom – is the modern-day euphemism for the toilet. Thus, in today's parlance, the name of this little town could be literally translated as *Holy Mary in the Toilet.* I was once rash enough to attempt this linguistic joke but received such dark and hostile looks that I never tried it again. I was made to feel like some latter-day pagan Visigoth who had just invaded this deeply religious land with my vulgar attempts at humour. In point of fact, the name translates something like *Holy Mary Bathed by the Sea* - which sounds far less blasphemous and much closer to the spirit of the place.

In the summer months, Santa Maria al Bagno provides the inhabitants of the nearest town – Galatone – with an escape route to the sea. The cafés, bars and the one main restaurant – outstandingly good - are alive with the buzz of Galatonesi of all ages chatting to each other and eating ice cream – much as they would have done had they been in their own town, but with the added pleasure of being near the sparkling Ionian Sea.

Since the population of Galatone *(prounced Ga LA toné)* consists of 16 000 inhabitants who comfortably fit 350 people into each square kilometre, it is a good thing that they do not all visit Santa Maria al Bagno in one go. The little beach, however, which is a natural sandy bay, must exceed the figure of 350 in the height of summer. Just how the Salentini love it - being huddled together and gregarious!

Galatone – once a Greek speaking town – has its attractions if you look for them. The main archway into the *centro storico* is possibly more alluring than the old town itself. But there are some ancient churches dotted around the town which shed light on how previous generations felt about God in that by-gone era.

I have more friends in Galatone than in any other town in Italy. I taught English to the aforementioned twin sisters, Diletta and Corrine, who went on to complete their studies at two of the most prestigious universities in Rome. They – and many others – give the lie to the notion that Southern Italians are lazy and possibly a bit dim-witted, as some ill-informed northerners would have you believe.

Back to Santa Maria al Bagno. If you visit it during off-peak times or in the usually sunny winter season, it is a haven of peace. Its little white buildings curve round the bay in a dignified loop as the sea laps contentedly on the rocks. It is reminiscent of the Greek seaside port that it must have originally been. Somehow, the native inhabitants, coffee bar owners and *restaurateurs* – plus one small general shop - survive throughout the year. You will be tempted to linger there and look in the estate agent's window, wondering if you have just come across the perfect place to retire to. Many do!

I always experience that *frisson* of real pleasure whenever I round the bend and set eyes on Santa Maria al Bagno again after intervals of some years, in the certain knowledge that is has not changed with time - nor fallen victim to the false gods of progress.

You loop round the bay and head off to the next resort which is called Santa Caterina. She too must have been bathed by the sea – but the coastline becomes rocky again, so she would have had to scrabble down to the water and launch herself into the depths of the Ionian Sea from some rocky spur. You become aware of how deep the sea is again – we once witnessed a gigantic lone mammal, a dolphin I believe, ducking and diving in the swell of the blue waters. It was a regular visitor to Santa Caterina, we were told.

There are lots of classy new bars and an excellent ice cream parlour at Santa Caterina. This little resort comes into its own at dusk as the sun goes down over the horizon and the street lamps light up the bars and restaurants to reveal a magic town at the foot of the towering black cliffs above. However, I remember Santa Caterina for its 'summer residences' hidden amongst the pine-tree covered hillsides; fantastical houses with Salento chimney stacks atop their flat rooves or palaces designed like Arabian follies standing empty in the winter months like neglected spirits in a state of limbo.

I once left my mobile phone there while my soul-mate and I were sitting on the grass-covered cliff tops above the sea. We had reached home in Sannicola by the time I missed it. She insisted that we returned to the spot – she driving my Panda along the narrow coastal roads as if we had been on the race track at Monza. At that point in my simple untechnical life, I had never conceived of the obvious procedure of trying to phone my number from her mobile. Thus we discovered my phone under a tuft of long grass – like a neglected pet hamster crying out for attention.

But the real jewel in the crown is still to come. You will need to appreciate the layout of Santa Caterina's one-way system, designed to avoid collisions in the summer months. You can return to Santa Caterina along the short coastal road from the north – where we want to be – but you cannot go north out of Santa Caterina along the same road. You need to drive uphill and turn sharp left near the top before going all the way downhill again until you reach the aforementioned coastal road.

The trip is worth it because you will come across the pine-tree-covered park and unspoilt rocks and beaches of Porto Selvaggio – the Wild Port - where you can once again encounter the Ionian Sea on the very edge of Paradise on Earth.

Your first visit to Porto Selvaggio should be experienced out of season – which is all year round except late July and August. There will be room to park your car and get out and visit this spot on foot; room to lose yourself in the cool forest and wonder at the stretches of pearlescent waters below. It is simply all sky, sparkling seas and air permeated by the smell of ozone and pine trees. The guardian of this magic place is an imposing watchtower which stands high above the sea. This is the tower which, if you recall, can be seen from the town of Gallipoli way down south. It is called *Il Torre dell'Alto* and it was originally built as an early-warning look-out post to alert the inhabitants of imminent hostile invaders – usually the Turks. Porto Selvaggio can also be reached along the main road out of Santa Caterina if ever you should miss the sharp left turn directly down to the coast.

The advantage of rejoining the coastal road is that it leads to a circular promontory where you can park your car and scramble up the hillside to reach the watchtower within the space of five breathless minutes, whilst never leaving sight of the endless stretch of sea beneath you. I have stood on this spot many times, alone or with friends and family – and on occasions in the intimate company of my *anima gemella (soulmate)* who shall remain nameless - making eternal promises and creating castles and watchtowers in the air, in defiance of invading Turks or even the realities of everyday life.

The road, by the way, simply peters out at this juncture, so you can devote your attention entirely to this place of refuge and head upwards towards the *Torre dell'Alto* on foot.

Once you reach the top of the cliff, you are free from traffic and noise. You can enjoy the sound of human voices. For there are always walkers, scout and guide outings – doing their equivalent of a Duke of Edinburg Award - families and romantic couples up there. But the spot never gets overcrowded.

Walk through the pine woods in peace and find the rock-hewn steps which descend to the beach below. The waters are clean and shallow enough to walk out towards the Ionian Sea in safety. But it is cold water. There is a fresh water spring that emerges from underground and spills out into sea from beneath the rocks.

Once, I took my elder son and his family to this spot. It was the highlight of their visit – well, apart from the food and wine we consumed at the *Villa Donna Isabella* just outside Sannicola, which might have made *Porto Selvaggio* a close second best.

On that occasion, however, I spent an angry thirty minutes clearing the pebbly beach of a mass of litter which had accumulated from the last summer season. Nobody had thought to clear up the unsightly mess until I arrived, outraged that people could visit this beauty spot and abuse it in such a manner. The few Italians who were present on the beach at the time merely looked on in bewilderment at this angry old English codger who charged around the beach muttering colourful Anglo-Saxon expletives as he set about his task. Not one of them offered to help.

Well, I warned you this would be Puglia with the gloves off. But I felt much better by the time I joined my son and grand-daughters in the sea. My daughter-in-law had decided she preferred to enjoy the pine-scented air and the tranquil azure sea from the relative comfort of the beach.

The local visitors to this spot are more likely to come from neighbouring Nardò. This might explain their strange reluctance to assist me in cleaning up their local beauty spot. Let me explain my tenuous theories on the subject of Nardò.

On first appearances, Nardò is a pleasant town with all its monuments – including a very elegant *castello* – in the right places. Its historical centre is imposing and at least equal to many other town centres in Salento. A very engaging romantic comedy called *Sei mai stata sulla luna?* was filmed in and around the picturesque historical centre of Nardò. (*'Have you ever been to the Moon?'* is the translation)

So what is it about Nardò I can't quite put my finger on? I recently went back with an English friend and colleague in search of a superb local restaurant called the *Hosteria Corte di Santa Lucia.* I had been introduced to this place by Italian friends from Sannicola. It specialises in local Salento cuisine and deserves more than its Tripadvisor four-star rating. But my friend and I tried for a fruitless hour-and-a-half to locate this restaurant in a town you can walk round in under thirty minutes. Asking the locals achieved very little, as they reacted to our questions in evasive manner. It wasn't that they were hostile – but inexplicably guarded. Some shrugged. Others claimed they weren't sure where it was. One girl told us she thought it had closed for the holidays. Another man sent us on a wild goose chase up a series of labyrinthine side streets. Why, we wondered, was our innocent enquiry so problematic? We ended up eating in a sandwich bar.

I do not want to prejudice you against this town because the inhabitants of Nardò do not deserve it. Suffice to relate that I know of a doctor from Bologna who wanted to buy a second home in Salento. She was ready to sign the final document which would have secured her dream house in the *centro storico* of Nardò. She was astounded and deeply disturbed to be told out of the blue at the eleventh hour that the house was no longer available for sale. The estate agent looked scared out of his wits. An unidentified individual had ordered the termination of the purchasing contract. It was in Nardò too where a farmer had 620 olives trees cut down overnight with a chain saw because he had refused to pay his *pizzo* to the local mafia clan. Need I say more?

But Salento has a charm and a dignity that transcends and predates by centuries the invisible but pervasive presence of the darker side of Italian life. Bear in mind too that foreigners and visitors are **immune**. Please show solidarity towards the people of Nardò, who go about their seemingly normal daily lives whilst living in the shadows of a darker force. Who knows? You may even discover a restaurant called *Hosteria della Santa Lucia* where I and my friend failed. That really would make your visit worthwhile! Nardò *is* worth a visit from a cultural and historic point of view – even if you are not hungry!

5:   *Going south down the Ionian coast to Santa Maria di Leuca.*

There are many places to the north of this part of Salento which I have not yet fully explored – notably the beauty spot favoured by many Italian visitors, a lively coastal town called Porto Cesareo. There is an island there too evocatively called *Isola dei Conigli* - Rabbit Island – more renowned for its unspoilt beaches than its animal population nowadays.

"I might have seen a couple of wild rabbits," claimed Beppe, my friend from Turin, who spent a week in San Cesareo with his wife, Federica. 'Beppe' is the model for the *commissario* in the three of my novels set in Abruzzo. A dubious claim to fame in my humble opinion - but Beppe seems quite happy with his status.

"Are you certain you would *recognise* a rabbit which was not on your dinner plate?" I asked him.

"Ah, English sense of humour!" he commented with a contented smile that he had deciphered the subtlety of my words. I did not spoil the moment by telling him I was merely being sarcastic.

But for now, we are going to take the road out of Gallipoli which leads southward to a place called Santa Maria di Leuca – pronounced LAY-oo-ka – right down to the 'heel' of the boot - where the waters of the Ionian Sea meet the Adriatic Sea in one seamless mass of sparkling light. The Sun, I should point out, is present more often than not.

The *superstrada* is the most direct way to reach Leuca, but there are numerous off-shoots which lead to picturesque spots on the coast as well as a host of 'inland' towns and villages too. I write 'inland' with inverted commas because you are only ever at most twenty minutes or so away from either of the seas in any part of Salento.

A 'must-go-to' visit is a coastal village called **San Gregorio**, because it is a truly unspoilt location of simple beauty. I always head for San Gregorio because I am unable to resist the imperative finger of the signpost pointing to this hidden treasure of Salento.

It was in this part of Salento where I was first taken by my Italian girlfriend to an old monastery – lost in the Salentino countryside not far from a seaside resort called Torre San Giovanni. There *were* a few cars there because otherwise there would have been nobody apart from the one surviving monk, who lived the life of a recluse, briefly spotted tending his fruit and olive trees behind the cloistered walls of a secret garden that belonged to God and the local sprites who still inhabit this ancient land. The chapel was claustrophobically saintly. A collection box fitted with an ancient padlock was, I suspect, the incumbent's only source of income. I'm not sure whether this place even had a name. But I will make enquiries and reveal its secret location later on. It was a time-warp experience – one of many during my haphazard discovery of Salento.

By the time you draw level with San Gregorio you will only be a short distance away from Santa Maria di Leuca. One more little town to be explored, on the left-hand side of the *superstrada* as you head south, is called Patù. On the map, the town name is underlined in blue – meaning a place of 'particular beauty or interest'. It is misleading looking it up on the internet because the whole page is full of photos of San Gregorio and the coastline – giving the impression that Patù is on the coast rather than a few kilometres inland. Patù will astonish you in its own right. Just to get matters into perspective, this small town was founded about 900 years before Jesus was born, by the Messapic people fleeing from Saracen invaders.

I am told you should also visit a neighbouring town called Morciano di Leuca. I haven't been there yet. Next time I am down that way, I surely will.

It is an awesome responsibility recommending places to visit – especially in Salento. But I don't believe I am misleading you. Every place I have talked about so far took me by surprise as soon as I set eyes upon them – even poor old Mancaversa! But you will discover other towns, villages, secret coves, watery grottoes and quaint churches which I have not yet discovered.

I have no qualms about pointing you in the direction of San Gregorio however. Out of season, it is a sleepy, tranquil spot, whose brightly painted houses – some inhabited all year round, indistinguishable from those which are summer homes only - slope down towards the rocky shore, as if ready to tumble into the Ionian Sea at the slightest push.

There is a sandy beach just beyond the village if you look northwards. May, June, early July and September are the best months to visit this part of the world. San Gregorio is, officially, part of Patù – being designated *La marina di Patù* – so you shouldn't see one without the other. Hidden under-the-surface grottoes are there to tempt serious divers – and I am reliably informed that the sunsets there are breath-taking. Naturally, you will eat well in San Gregorio – especially seafood.

As of recently, I know one couple who live there permanently. They have a remarkable daughter graced with the name of Doriana, who spent her formative years in San Gregorio. Doriana is now in her thirties – an intellectual and spiritual nomad. She is to my mind a true *folletto salentino* from top to toe – and as far as I can tell, still in her formative years. But more of Doriana later on! I should explain that *un folletto* translates as 'a sprite' – but I thought I should write the Italian word because it sounds so apt in the context. Doriana is a convert to Veganism, by the way. I was not surprised to learn about this aspect of her character. Somehow it could not have been otherwise – as she blazes her elusive and modest trail wherever she goes. She gives herself unreservedly to all living creatures and wishes no harm to any soul. It is currently possible to meet her in person where she works; but more of that in a later chapter.

Other inland towns should be visited apart from Patù, Morciano di Leuca – Salve being one of them. But take your time, because the whole point about Salento is that its charm and character rarely strike one straight away. I have, I seem to remember, already spoken about the magic of Salento creeping up on you surreptitiously. And I haven't got round to talking about their *feste* yet, where you will be transported to another era altogether by local musicians and a bewitching dance called the *Pizzica*.

We are going to head for Santa Maria di Leuca now – a short drive away from San Gregorio. It has an attractive port, although I have always found the town itself a bit puzzling, as if it is not sure how it should react to its unique position. But the important thing about Leuca is that you have reached the actual heel of Italy's boot. You may have been to Land's End in Cornwall – but that is nothing! Leuca calls itself *Finibus Terrae* – Land's End, of course, but how much more evocative the words sound in Latin!

My first visit to Santa Maria di Leuca was with my Italian girlfriend. Let's call her Rosaria, as I did in my first three novels, of which she is the 'reluctant' heroine. She was my tour guide in the days when she felt it her mission in life to open up the mysteries of Salento to this displaced soul who had somehow arrived from some obscure village outside London, wearing a burgundy-coloured jacket and a green cardigan. She took me clothes shopping early on in our relationship - claiming she could not be seen in public with any man who was dressed like I was – from which I emerged wearing jeans for the first time (late) in my life. The cardigan and burgundy jacket were unceremoniously dumped in a passing street bin without my say-so. Thus began this new era in my life.

The first thing she told me as she drove resolutely up towards the lighthouse end of *Finibus Terrae* was that the road surfaces had all been repaired prior to the visit of Pope Benedict – way back at the beginning of this century. They had even built a helicopter pad on a cliff top near the town so His Holiness could fly down directly from the Vatican. I have nothing against popes, by the way – being a semi-convinced Catholic myself. But I commented at the time that it was amazing how public funds could magically appear out of thin air when the need materialised.

The roads *were* in a healthier state than in the rest of Salento, it was true. I have to make the point, however, that road surfaces have been largely put to rights in Salento in the second decade of the 21st century – probably thanks to tourism - and are now in a better condition than they are in the present-day Disunited Kingdom of 2019.

We drove uphill and parked round a wide and airy *piazza* where stands the Basilica dedicated to The Virgin Mary. The basilica is officially designated *un santuario* – a shrine or a sanctuary, of course - where mere mortals can escape from the sometimes grim realities of life. There is an obelisk in the centre of the *piazza* which looks as if it is struggling to match in height the lighthouse which stands guard over the deep waters of the two seas.

This part of Leuca *is* truly beautiful with carefully tended stone steps leading down to the colourful port and marina down below on the Ionian side of the town.

I was led, literally by the hand, from the Ionian side of the *piazza* towards the Adriatic side. Of course, Sicily is much further south than Puglia, but it was a sobering thought that North Africa was the next land mass one would encounter by travelling southwards. Leuca's imposing lighthouse marks the boundary between two diverse cultures – as well as having the task of warning ships of the impending dangers posed by this rocky peninsular.

What a contrast between the Ionian side and the eastward facing view across the Adriatic. Looking northwards, the mighty cliffs disappear into the shimmering blue distance, lapped by the azure waters of the Adriatic as far as the eye can see.

I glanced over the solid protective wall and looked down the sheer drop of the cliff. To my surprise, I noticed an elegant new stone building at the base by the water's edge. It appeared to be only accessible by boat. I pointed it out to Rosaria. I shall always remember her exact words.

"Ah, yes. I read about that," she said. "It's *abusivo* – built by 'those people' who I was telling you about."

"You mean the Sacra Corona U...."

Rosaria raised a stern finger as she cast her eyes around to make sure nobody was close enough to us to have overheard the forbidden words that I was thoughtlessly uttering. It brought home to me the extent to which the inhabitants of this part of the world live in fear of the shadowland that exists in a parallel universe to their own. I vividly recall a similar incident on a Ryanair flight to Pescara at a later stage in my travels. I was chatting to a young couple sitting next to me. They were heading for Foggia – a town in the north of Puglia. They were telling me that they wanted to escape from their town and go and live and work in 'free' London. This, of course, was before that monumental political, cultural and economic blunder was committed in allowing a referendum on our continued membership of the EU on June 23rd 2016.

"In Foggia," whispered Alessia, "we have the mafia!"

"Oh, you mean the Sacra Corona…" I began, lowering my voice on this occasion but wanting her to know that I was *au fait* with the darker side of life in Italy.

The couple looked horrified and fearful – despite the roar of two jet engines and a healthy buzz of conversation all round us – *Quod Erat Demonstrandum,* I fear.

Rosaria and I took refuge inside the *Santuario* – God's territory under the auspices of the Pope in its earthly guise. Rosaria dipped her fingers into the holy water stoop and made a silent sign of the cross to banish all evil before we did a reverential tour of the inside of the church.

* * *

Respects paid to the Good Lord, we were soon travelling up north along the Adriatic coast, high above sea level on the coastal road. If you continue along this stretch of coastline, you will ultimately reach the ancient town of Otranto, which is pronounced unusually with the stress on the initial 'O'. However, that was not our destination for today. We crossed a modern bridge which spanned a deep but narrow ravine. We had arrived at a spot called *La baia di Ciolo* – the Bay of Ciolo, pronounced '**cho**-lo'.

It was out of season, so there were few people to spoil the atmosphere of this isolated beauty spot. We found a place to park with ease. I remember being struck by the smell of the ocean and the perfume of wild herbs on the breeze, as we stood on the clifftop looking down on the turquoise waters below.

Alarmingly, Rosaria seemed to be carrying a bag containing towels and swimwear – including my trunks. Surely she wasn't intending for us to go swimming in this vast expanse of water? The sea suddenly looked deeply menacing beneath the sparkling surface. Swimming was, it transpired, part of the programme she had in mind.

As we crossed back over the bridge to reach the steps that led down to the cove, Rosaria told me in complete seriousness that in the summer the local teenagers made a sport of jumping off the bridge vertically, feet first, into the waters below.

"You mean they wish to commit suicide?" I asked only half-jokingly.

If I was inclined to disbelieve her, I witnessed the living proof that it was true with my own eyes on a later visit. Do Italian males – drivers and divers – have a secret desire to end it all in one single act of bravado? I still believe it can be explained by the absence of the 'future gene' in their psychological make-up, as previously mentioned. Italians are much better adapted than Anglo-Saxons at living entirely for the present – although a remarkable Italian physicist named Carlo Ravelli has convinced me entirely, via his book called *The Order of Time,* that the Present is too brief - a fraction of a nanosecond - to be perceived by the human brain. The Present simply does not exist, according to this gentleman, since we are in a state of continuous and unceasing change.

On that memorable day with Rosaria, there were maybe six other people on the 'beach' – which consisted of a sloping concrete area which led to the water's edge. Behind us, a footpath led up the deep gully on to the grassy slopes above – a refuge for the modest ones who wanted to change into swimming gear – or vice versa. The waters in the bay were clean and unpolluted and widened out into the bay after a few metres of rock pools – full of little fish darting about in the rippling sunlight. In the height of summer, the sole form of pollution is a film of suntan lotion that floats on the surface where the water is still shallow.

Rosaria did not think to ask me if I could swim – she took it for granted. What she did not know was that I had never really swum out of my depth before. If I ever had, it would have been a simple matter of a few strokes shoreward to find my footing on the sand beneath. Like any typical male, my pride would not let me admit to such a weakness. It rapidly became apparent that Rosaria swam like a mermaid. I had to concentrate on not thinking about how deep the waters were below me and just continued with my steady breaststroke. After a few minutes, I realised I would probably make it to the ledge of rock we were heading for some 200 metres out into the bay. When it was all over, I felt exhilarated by what I had achieved. I felt the thrill of defying death – in the most beautiful setting I have ever known in my life. Having said this, I should confess that I have hardly ever ventured further than France, Italy and Greece - apart from one trip to Western Australia to visit my younger son and his family.

When we arrived at the 'beach', I told Rosaria that it was the first time I had swum out of my depth.

"Why didn't you tell me you aren't a strong swimmer, Ric?" she scolded me. "I might have lost you."

"Ah, but you didn't, did you?" I told her defiantly.

After Ciolo, we made our way back home, not retracing our steps but attempting the cross-country route. At one point, the signposts gave out and Rosaria had to ask directions of an old lady wearing black. She spoke only dialect so I could not understand what she was saying. Rosaria explained that the old woman had confessed to her that she had never once left her village in her whole life – thereby implying she was unable to tell us which road to take. There are elderly people in Salento, as in many rural areas of Italy, where this is still true in the 21st century. I was moved.

I have been back two or three times to Ciolo. The last time was with my elder son and his family. The wooden shack that was the *trattoria* when I first visited the bay with Rosaria has now been converted into a much smarter and larger wooden shack! My daughter-in-law ordered the best sea-food pasta dish that I had never tasted! I was frustrated because I had ordered some 'inferior' dish of clams just to avoid having to pull the meat off the prawns. Apart from responding to increasing numbers of tourists, this eating place has not changed at all over the course of this century. *Grazie a Dio!* Take your time eating as you look out over the Adriatic Sea down below and breathe in the scent of wild thyme and sage wafted on the breeze.

6:   *Otranto and trekking in Salento*

My life in Salento is divided into two parts – 2001 until 2009 and 2010 until the present day i.e. 2021. We are now officially blighted by this ridiculous mess called Brexit. Most of our cultural, social and trade links are severed – to a greater or lesser extent. The abandonment of Erasmus is a criminal act enacted against the intelligent young of our nation. Whilst a buffoon called Boris sails blithely on making blunder after blunder. It just has to be the hugest political mistake in the history of England. In 2009, I made *my* biggest mistake; I returned to the United Kingdom. I won't go into the motives for my return to my Buckinghamshire Village but they seemed valid at the time. Now, I am desperately working out how I can return permanently to Puglia. My friends and colleagues from my teaching days never tire of telling me that I should have stayed where I was. I tell them, feebly, that it wasn't that simple. At least I managed to write eight novels – all set in Italy – over the intervening decade. Distance lends perspective maybe.

Until 2019, I returned to the land of my soul's desire at great cost to myself with flights to and from Brindisi, Ryanair looking a bit shaky, rocketing car rental prices and the outrageous sums of money needed to take a reasonable supply of essentials in a reasonably sized suitcase to see me through my stay. But I digress – yet again!

Otranto and trekking in Salento belong to the first half of the century. Although I have been back to Otranto with my family and joined the trekking group on the Sundays when I have been on holiday. But there is something contradictory about constantly going on holiday to the place where you know you ought to be living permanently. It prevents one going on holiday to other destinations – a willingly self-imposed restriction, I have to admit.

If I say to you, "You must visit Otranto" it sounds as if I am ordering you to include this ancient settlement on your list of essential places to visit; which I am in a way. NOT to visit it once would be a dereliction of duty. Let me explain.

You will not be disappointed by this town. Not going there would be akin to a foreign visitor going to London and not seeing Big Ben or Tower Bridge. But tourists from all over the globe abound in Otranto ever since the 21st century got under way.

Before you set off, you might – if like me you are a stickler for the correct pronunciation – want to practise saying **O**tranto as the Italians pronounce it – with the stress on the first syllable. I'm being pedantic, of course, but I become infuriated by presenters of travel and house buying programmes on the TV who never bother to find out the correct local pronunciation of place names before they go on air.

Transport from Lecce to Otranto is good. The famous Sud-Est trains run from Lecce to Otranto regularly – calling at all stations on the way. You might even consider getting off at Corigliano d'Otranto on the way – just to admire its ancient castle and the shady *piazza* where the local market is held. Corigliano is actually not on the doorstep of Otranto, despite its name.

In the summer months, there are well-organised 'colour coded' coaches (Un 'pullman' in Italian) which go to various destinations in Salento, including Otranto on a more-or-less daily basis. The main tourist office in the Piazza Sant' Oronzo will help you; the staff all speak excellent English and are genuinely eager to please. After all, the reputation of their beloved Salento is at stake. Young people might have to leave Salento for the sake of a career but their affection for the homeland is heart-warmingly convincing. I know one such girl who now lives and works in Woking. Micaela is living happily with an Englishman and their first child. But she 'dragged' her future husband back to Gallipoli – entirely willing to be dragged – to get married in that cathedral.

Otranto – which is among the oldest towns you will ever visit – has history coming out of every pore. But it has become a little too 'touristy' as the 21st Century has progressed – which was why I hesitated to endorse it outright at the beginning of the chapter. It has avoided becoming gaudy – or over-priced like Venice. As you walk through the entrance to the old town, its 'oldness' will strike you. It is, literally, massively old.

Even the new town is not unattractive and the protected beach is clean and well managed. You can eat seafood till your heart's content in both the old and the new town. Otranto is the first place where I ordered seafood pasta cooked in 'black ink' from the squid. Delicious in risotto form too.

When I first visited Otranto in 2001, its imposing castle was closed to the public on that day. The town was full of local Italians who used to make it the destination for their Sunday outing. In the latter part of the first two decades, Salento has woken up to the fact that tourists are a necessary element of economic life. So the old castle-cum-stronghold stands a better chance of being open.

But the site which holds the most powerful memories for me is the Cathedral-Basilica tucked away in a side street and dedicated to the Annunciation of the Blessed Virgin Mary. It has the most beautiful crypt I have ever visited. It was originally Rosaria who insisted I go and see this place. She was always an assiduous and well-informed guide. The most outstanding feature in the whole church is the monument dedicated to the Martyrs of Otranto – massacred by the Turks because they refused to renounce their Christian faith. The massacre took place on 14 August 1480. 813 inhabitants were murdered by the invading heathens.

Their skeletons – not all 813 I would reckon – are on display in an upright position, side by side, behind three tall glass cabinets which reach up to the arched ceiling above. You are left gazing at them wondering what they must have looked like when they were alive. This seemingly grotesque spectacle, from another era altogether - when humans were obliged to be much less squeamish about death - brings home the pain and suffering endured by those who held firm religious beliefs over the centuries. It is a salutary reminder that history is repeating itself in many countries even in this, the 21st century AD. Their courage and faith must be an inspiration to those visitors who stare at this monument with muted horror.

I have fond memories of another trip to Otranto, not of the town itself but in the countryside and coastal paths just half a kilometre or so to the south. In my early days in Salento, I joined a group of trekkers who call themselves *Speleo Trekking Salento.* I am still an honorary member even today. You will find details of this trekking group on the internet – with many photos of its founder member – a healthy and immensely sociable Salentino gentleman called Riccardo. Tragically, he lost his wife, Rita, an equally jovial lady barely in her fifties, to cancer. She too would energetically stride around Salento in the company of the often one hundred-strong group of fellow walkers. I have vivid memories of stopping amidst the olive trees while the stragglers caught up – the gap between the various factions finally closing up. A short-lived event, since as soon as we were all reunited, the leaders would shoot off again at a healthy pace, leaving the same stragglers to straggle again.

On this occasion, we were trekking along the rough coastal path passing wide sandy coves exposed to the dazzling waters of the Adriatic Sea. We were heading for the lighthouse some four or five kilometres distant. We must have looked a suspicious bunch – certainly not decked out in our Sunday best. We became aware that a boat belonging to the *Guardia Costale (Coast Guard police)* was coming in close to the shore and sounding a klaxon to boot! Riccardo – probably – scrambled down the rocks towards the boat. To everybody's amusement, it transpired that we had been mistaken for a group of illegal immigrants from Albania.

We made it to the lighthouse and devoured our packed lunches, sitting in the heather or perched on rocks. We had been promised a visit inside the lighthouse by an official. Obviously, his wife had not allowed him to skip the

Sunday lunch she had been at pains to prepare – a sacrosanct moment all over Italy, but especially so in the deep south.

The lighthouse keeper's lunch was obviously going to be a protracted affair. I can imagine that he undertook the guided tour in good faith, *Speleo Trekking Salento* being a highly respected organisation. But his wife obviously put her foot firmly down. A group of us decided that we were not going to wait for his arrival, so we finished our packed lunches and headed back to the starting point via a different route. We accidently discovered a well-known 'beauty spot' where the iron-rich red cliffs descended to a tranquil green lake – the two colours creating an unusual visual effect. I had been taken there before by the school secretary Emanuela and her *fidanzato,* Claudio. I believe I had been rather dismissive of this spectacle in my early days, telling Claudio it was only a jumped-up quarry pit. I was wrong – it is an entirely natural phenomenon. I appreciated it much more on this my second visit but would not consider it as an essential part of Salento's natural heritage. But I regretted the fact that I had been so dismissive.

But there is a splendid *agriturismo* nearby called *La Torre di Marta* – Martha's Tower - which definitely does fall into the category of Salento's heritage. Marta is the owner's name and she runs it with her sisters. Marta was in her fifties even way back at the beginning of the century. She and her sisters personally cook and smilingly deliver to the tables dish after dish of vegetables, fish and meat in a seemingly endless succession of simple culinary delights. As is usually the case in an *agriturismo,* there is no menu – thus removing at a stroke the often painful process of eliminating one tasty-sounding dish in favour of another. You eat outdoors in the shade of a pergola covered with creeping vines. In England, there is no real equivalent – and you would have paid 'an eye of the head' for such a feast. By legal definition, rarely ignored but not necessarily adhered rigidly to, you cannot call it an *agriturismo* unless 60% of the food is home produced. That usually includes the ducks, chickens and rabbits etc - a brilliant Italian invention to be found in abondance all over the Peninsula.

* * *

Going up the coast from Santa Maria di Leuca, there are countless resorts and stop-off places along the way. The cliffs and rocky inlets progressively become sandy beaches and low, rocky shorelines, until you reach San Cataldo. San Cataldo is back on the level with Lecce – and it is where many Leccesi escape to when they wish to breathe in the sea air, and eat seafood at any one of the excellent restaurants there.

At any point along the endless coastline, you can usually park up and visit the sea, the beaches or the rocky promontories jutting out into the Adriatic Sea. But avoid late July and August if you can. You'll be lucky to find a spot to park a bicycle let alone an SUV – or a towel, come to that.

One of my favourite places going up the coastline is Castro. It is open to the elements and excellent outdoor eating places abound. I make special mention of a little rocky bay evocatively called Zinzalusa, where I was taken by my mermaid other half, as previously hinted at. Not that she sports a fish's tail as soon as she is submerged – but I have rarely come across anyone who looked so completely in her natural element in deep water. I dived into the water off a rock and followed her with my erratic breast-stroke, suppressing the panic swelling up when I realised I could not actually see the sea bed at all. But we reached a magic, echo-filled grotto where the cold clear waters never see the sun's rays. We probably shouted amorous declarations just for the weird experience of hearing our magnified voices reverberating round the rocky walls. When we swam back to our starting point, I had to be ignominiously hauled out of the water on to the flat rock above by a couple of young lads who were fortuitously present – laughing at my discomfort in amiable manner. They carried out the operation to please my beautiful companion rather than out of any desire to save my life, I suspect.

On that occasion, after having been rescued from the depths of the Adriatic Sea, we headed back westwards towards Casarano. Rosaria wanted to show me an ancient chapel in a pine wood on the road back towards Maglie. I shall never forget that little detour. As we were heading back towards our car, we noticed a gathering of young men who had just arrived. They all wore designer sunglasses and Rolex watches. They had arrived in brand new Audis – inevitably Audis! Rosaria was looking petrified. I immediately understood to what strata of Puglian society these individuals belonged. It was a secret, unofficial mafia reunion.

"We must leave NOW, Ric!" Rosaria whispered fearfully.

Brave and foolhardy me – after my unimpressive performance of being hauled out of the sea – took hold of Rosaria's hand and marched her past the sinister gathering talking loudly in English. Rosaria's dark olive skin must surely have given the game away – she simply could not have been remotely English. Once in the car, she shot out of the woods like an arrow back to the 'safety' of the main road. I doubt we were in any real danger, but Rosaria's reaction brought home to me yet again the underlying fear of the 'mafia' which can be unleashed when one physically crosses the border between these two parallel worlds.

I must emphasise – visitors are never in any danger. But if you truly wish to understand the undercurrents in this part of the world, then you should be aware of the usually invisible and unobtrusive presence of the criminal underworld – so often invisibly linked to everyday activities. It is a fact that the clans are often responsible for refuse collection – having acquired the contracts quite legally. It explains why the dustmen never go on strike – unless ordered to do so by the local boss. You will not cross the great divide – neither do the vast majority of Italians – but if you want to understand how aspects of Italian life really work, then you should at least be aware of the undercurrents.

If you ask local people if the mafia is present in their part of Puglia, they will go into denial mode; they will tell you areas where the mafia *does* exist – which are *never* on their doorstep. *L'Omertà* – the code of silence, comes into play.

Life, after all, must go on; people buy cars, eat out, go to work, visit the hairdresser, raise their families and send their sons and daughters to university. They are far more willing to decry the vagaries of Italian politics than talk about the parallel world of the mafia. Incidentally, I have been struck since June 23rd 2016 how many seemingly intelligent, articulate Italians are envious of the UK's decision to leave the EU. Discontent about the Brussels power house is not confined to the UK, by any manner of means. I still believe they are passing judgement in the wrong direction. It is all too often a countries' politicians to blame for the perceived injustices in our lives.

* * *

I am going to conclude this chapter by mentioning other places which you might visit if you ever stay for a protracted period – or more likely feel driven to return on many subsequent occasions. My story is about to change tack. But I cannot do that without attempting to do justice to the countless other towns which lie between the Adriatic Coast and Lecce. The 'list' is in random order. One more word of grateful acknowledgement dedicated to Speleo Trekking Salento, without whom I would never have discovered the vast swathes of unspoilt countryside in Puglia, the little roadside shrines dedicated to the mother of Christ, the rustic eating places along the way and the free history lessons on every pile of stones we came across in the midst of olive groves – and the inevitably genial company of educated and friendly *Salentini*. *Mille grazie, STS!*

Tricase – a friendly town with an important hospital run by Catholic nuns. I once turned up there without an appointment because I had the symptoms of a detached retina. I told a doctor and he treated me on the spot, free of charge. God bless Italy, I thought.

Helen Mirren owns a restored *masseria* nearby but has recently fallen foul of the local planning authorities – even the rich and famous are not exempt from pernickety planning committees, it seems. I am unsure of the details – this was a bit of hearsay from someone I met – *una brava persona*, no doubt! Whenever an Italian tells you that someone is *una brava persona*, you may semi-reliably infer that the person concerned is trustworthy, honest, direct in his or her dealings - basically not a crook like everyone else who they don't know personally! It's always 'who-you-know' which counts in Italian life.

Maglie is a busy and prosperous town vying with Lecce to be the economic centre of Salento. Benedetto Cavalieri has a pasta factory there. His dried pasta is of an exceptional quality and renowned all over Italy. That's official, by the way - I'm not inventing this. I had the honour of teaching

English at Salento University in the company of his wife, who held a permanent English teaching post in the *Beni Culturali* faculty.

Maglie is also home to an internationally famous brand of chocolates – Maglio di Maglie *Gambero Rosso*. This means 'Red Lobster" – which I cannot explain in chocolate terms. The company was founded in 1875. I am told these chocolates are on sale in Harrods as well as being renowned all over Italy. Yes, you can call both enterprises up on the internet for further mouth-watering information.

The towns belonging to the GRECIA SALENTINA region.

This is the area of Salento where the dialect called GRIKO is spoken – a variation of Greek, as I mentioned at the beginning of this account. They are old Greek settlements dating back centuries. Any or all of these towns are worthy of your attention for their beautifully preserved architecture and above all their cultural richness. They are dotted around between Maglie – including this town - and Otranto. Looking them up on the internet is a frustrating business since most of the photos are of the spectacular coastline north and south of Otranto. All of the towns are inland – although nowhere in Salento is very far from the coast – as I feel it necessary to emphasise.

Whichever of these towns you decide to visit, may I implore you to see at least one of them after dark? They take on a magic all of their own when the little *piazze* and the old stone churches are aglow with the yellow light reflected from the Leccese stone walls. Not only that, but evening time is when the local population comes to life. Try to find out in advance when their local Feast Day is held. Many of these *feste* supply you with inexpensive street food of a very high standard – not just in Grecia Salentina, of course.

I will mention **Melpignano** next because this is where the annual **Notte della Taranta** takes place in August. This is the musical event where you will see and hear the **Pizzica** – and other folk dances - being played and danced until dawn.

Giurdignano and Muro Leccese. Both of these towns are situated just off the main road between Otranto and Maglie. Giurdignano is the smaller of the two towns. The town itself is worthy of a visit. Its ancient architecture is beautifully preserved. But the site is among the oldest in Italy – going back to the Bronze Age. The unspoilt countryside surrounding the town is the site of dolmen and Megalithic standing stones which bring home to us just how steeped in history this part of Italy is. You really do get a sense of the past merely by breathing the air and soaking up the atmosphere of the place.

Muro Leccese – OK! Stop! I know this book is supposed to be a kind of travel guide, but it's also a personal account of what Puglia / Salento has done for me. And, I hope, what it will do for you!

So, I have just had a thought. Here's an idea for you to mull over. Why not make this beautiful town the centre point for your exploration of Salento? If you have a car, it will be easier to park it than in the capital city of Salento – ie Lecce. You can spend two days visiting Lecce and then simply book yourself into one of the less expensive traditional hotels in Muro Leccese. Perhaps the *Villa Zaira* is a bit over the top; it usually hosts wedding receptions at about €100 per head – that's for the food only, I guess. Even that would be worth paying for just to bind your soul to another person's in such a simply spectacular manner – or manor, do I mean? Hotel prices in Salento make the natives gasp in horror. To us Brits, used to paying through the nose for a night's stay at Gatwick Airport, hotel prices in Puglia seem excessively modest. Even the biggest hotel in Lecce, the Hotel Tiziano, will do bed and breakfast for well under €100 a night.

Muro Leccese is a beautifully preserved old town which deserves days of attention for its own sake – but puts you within striking distance of all the places I have been describing. It's just an idea. For once, the internet photos of this town give an accurate picture of its splendid architecture. It is surrounded by enchanting countryside too. Go for the proper Italian web sites – not Tripadvisor, if you can avoid that pointless invasion from the other side of the Atlantic. Tripadvisor's hotel prices are inevitably more than if you phone up the hotel in person to make your bookings – in my experience, I should say!

I could go on for pages about all the other towns and places to visit. But I guess you've got the message by now.

I shall pluck two more places out of the air almost at random. After that, this account is going to change tack. The first is a place called **Acaya** – sometimes spelt Acaja. You need to find a town called **Vèrnole** and head north for a short distance. Acaya comes under the jurisdiction of Vernole. I did visit this place during the dawn of this century – I am not sure I fully appreciated its significance at the time. The massive castle and the village have been restored since I visited the town. It is an outstanding example of a medieval fortified town. The interior streets crisscross each other in a symmetric manner. The castle was designed by the same architect/builder as the *Castello Carlo V* in Lecce. Apparently, the architect was found guilty of embezzling funds – of course, he *was* Italian – and ended up a prisoner in the castle he had designed, where he died ignominiously. If you are into history, then the details of this bit of historic story should fascinate you.

The second random choice of a 'monument' to Salento is just off the road returning to Brindisi. You are looking for a site called **Santa Maria di Cerrate**

This remarkable site has been restored – in fact the restoration of the site is ongoing. But funds have been officially invested since 2012 and restoration is well on the road to completion. I have to confess that I have not yet visited Santa Maria di Cerrate. But this visit is on top of my priority list next time. The site is well sign-posted along the road from Lecce to Brindisi. It is between the main road and the Adriatic coast – more or less opposite a town called Squinzano. Santa Maria di Cerrate is underlined in blue on the map – indicating a place of outstanding interest and natural beauty etc etc.

Here is a quote from the website – available in Italian and English. *www.fondoambiente.it/abbazia-di-santa-maria-di-cerrate-eng/*

Once a Greek orthodox monastery, then the centre of a farm, this notable example of Puglian Romanesque architecture now tells the tale of its two previous lives – one religious, the other agricultural.

Shrouded in mystery and immersed in the olive groves that cover the area outside the city of Lecce, the origins of the abbey complex can be traced back to Tancred, King of Sicily...

Take a look at the above official website – not the usual Tripadvisor one – but the official Italian one, I emphasise.

It just so happens that there is an outstanding *agriturismo,* within walking distance from Santa Maria di Cerrate, called the **Masseria Melcarne.** And yes, before you even think of asking, I have been there on three occasions – notably for my friend Rita's 60th birthday. The address of this place is **Strada Provinciale 93, Torre Rinalda.** It is about 5 kilometres outside a town called Surbo. Telephone number 0039 368 958 324.

When it describes the *masseria* as being 'immersed in olive groves' it is quite literally the case – but it is also immersed in its own farm land. The building itself forms part of Salento's history. When – not if – you go and eat here, you will never want to leave Salento again. Booking beforehand is essential. A Satnav is a good idea too! You could actually spend your whole holiday here if you so wished – they run cookery courses for the likes of you and me.

If you do decide to go to this *masseria* to have lunch or dinner, look out for *Ciceri e tria* - pasta with chick peas - and *Fave e ciccoria* – broad bean and potato purée with chicory. Both of these dishes are a Salento speciality. They also do pasta with a homemade olive purée sauce. I'm absolutely not saying you won't eat as well in countless similar establishments throughout Salento – but you may be hard-pushed to match the ambience of the *Masseria Melcarne*. Look up their website and you will see for yourself.

Just to round this chapter off: If you are leaving from - or indeed just arriving at – Brindisi airport, there is the most beautiful little church, barely a kilometre from the runway, called **Santa Maria del Casale**. It must have nearly got swallowed up by the airport, but luckily, the populace's inherent love of its traditions meant that it survived there in all its simple splendour. Ask at the petrol station just outside the airport where this church is – should you have missed the signpost for it. They will be highly impressed by your local knowledge. Strictly speaking, this church is outside the scope of this book – we are no longer in Salento at Brindisi Airport – but who cares - it's all Puglia, in any case!

7:   Dancing to the Pizzica

So far, we have moved from place to place – at times a bit haphazardly, I have to confess. Now is the time to concentrate on specific aspects of life down here in the south of Puglia – its traditional music, for example.

I shall talk about specific towns in Salento – not as a tourist but from the point of view of the people who live there. These are people - and places - which have had an impact on my life. There is a town called **Cutrofiano**, where I have returned every year since 2015. It is a very normal *cittadina* – a nice word for 'a small town' and the same as the word for one of its female inhabitants. It only has 12 000 inhabitants, which is a comfortable size sufficient to guarantee the presence of a weekly food, clothes and kitchen appliances market every Wednesday, two banks, three chemists, three bakers and several small but well-stocked supermarkets. It also happens to have the best homemade ice-cream parlour outside Lecce. It is situated some thirty kilometres to the south of Lecce and equidistant between the Adriatic and the Ionian seas. It's the kind of place where one could happily settle – and where a hardy handful of English people *have* settled – including a gentleman called Fred, who lives happily alongside the locals but has difficulty in forming a complete sentence in Italian – proving the point that it can be done!

In this short chapter, I will attempt to do justice to Salento's captivating folk music.

I'm sure you have heard of a dance called the Tarantella. It is an ancient dance, originally from Sicily, I believe, although its origins are shrouded in the mists of time. It first came into being for the sake of those who had been bitten by the tarantula – thus its name. The tempo of the music, played on crude instruments by locals, got faster and faster towards the end, until the 'victim' of the spider bite fell to the ground exhausted. I would assume that the increased heart rate and blood flow was instrumental in dispersing the poison. This tradition as with many others has its roots in poverty – just as the French used to eat snails because most of the populace could not afford meat. Born out of sheer necessity, the tradition becomes a sophisticated art form.

The peculiarly Salento version of this dance has come to be known as the Pizzica (pronounced **PEETZica)** which is derived from the word *'pizzicare'* which means to bite or to pinch in modern Italian; thus the connection with spiders.

I was bewildered by the number of similar sounding words in Italian when I first arrived:

Piazza – *a town square*

Pizza - *the thing you eat*

Pizzo - *protection money paid to the mafia*

Pizzetto - *a goatee beard*

Pizzaiolo – *a pizza maker*

And then the word **Pizzica** was added to my collection.

The Pizzica has evolved into an art form and constitutes the solid basis of Salentino folk music. It is occasionally danced as a courting ritual between a man and a woman. Physical contact between the dancers is unheard of. Nowadays, the dance is performed for the sheer pleasure of moving to its intoxicating rhythms. The music is often provided by men with a female vocalist in the role of the lead singer – but there are no rigid rules. It depends very much on the individual bands. Many of these bands have two girls in their teens or early twenties who dance to the live music, decked out in local costumes and, traditionally making patterns in the air with a red silk neck scarf as a prop. Often though, the silk scarf is absent, so that the performers can concentrate on the intricate dance steps. The band plays on a variety of instruments; guitars, tambourines, even a violin and inevitably – my favourite instrument of all – an accordion. But then there is that most vital instrument of all – the human voice.

I first witnessed the Pizzica being danced at an outdoor party which I had been invited to by a family of local lawyers who had taken me under their wing so to speak. The old Salento house had a spacious covered courtyard whose roof was supported by stone pillars overlooking a garden full of fig trees and other fruit trees in abundance – including *Nespole* trees. This is sweet fruit typical of southern Italy looking like an apricot and as sweet and sticky as a fig. You don't need to buy them at the supermarket – you just pick them off the trees as you find them.

And suddenly, there they were dancing and playing music which sounded completely alien to my English middle-class ears. It got under the skin. I couldn't get the music out of my head – even now, some twenty years later.

I even wrote my first novel and entitled it "Dancing to the Pizzica" – a kind of *giallo-romantico,* a romantic thriller. But the theme is far more to do with the clash of two cultures, a middle-class Englishman and a woman from Salento, whose way of thinking he has to come to terms with.

There is nothing like the Pizzica in England. The only traditional English dance that comes to mind is Morris Dancing. I have never been particularly turned on by the sight of men banging sticks together and raising their kneecaps in the air. Unfair, I know. But the Pizzica raises folk music on to another plane altogether. It has become a cult dance throughout Italy, with Pizzica classes springing up all over the country. It is an immensely captivating dance.

I have already mentioned the annual music festival in a town called Melpignano – *La Notte della Taranta*. This event is attended by thousands of spectators and a host of different musical groups from every corner of Puglia. The event is not limited to Melpignano; the festival 'tours' round Salento spending one night in each town during the summer months.

But whenever each town or village holds its annual saint's day festival and the colourfully lit white wooden arches are erected along the main streets, you will be able to witness the Pizzica being danced for the benefit of local people – tourists are always welcome too! Many villages provide street food on these occasions. It is as if each little town becomes one big family reunion such is the sense of 'belonging' created by the *feste*.

I was fortunate enough to get to know such a group of musicians in Sannicola (near Gallipoli) where I lived for six years. The group is called **Schiattacore** – meaning 'Heartbreak'. During the daytime, the head of family, Francesco Giaffreda, ran the local betting shop. The group is made up of family members. The lead singer is his daughter, Ylenia, who had just started studying music at the Università del Salento in Lecce. She also plays folk tunes on the violin. Her voice is perfectly adapted to the music – forthright, with an almost raucous edge to it which is essential to accompany the insistent, resonating beat of the music. She is only about 1 metre 50 tall but her amplified voice can fill town squares with vocal sounds from a long gone past.

How to describe the dance? It's an agile, skipping, lilting movement of the body – almost as if the feet hardly touch the ground. It is usually women who excel in executing the dance. The man, when present, will dance around the woman trying to entice and seduce her. I discovered a video of a boy about 12 on Youtube just yesterday who was billed as the youngest male dancer of the pizzica. He was doing it brilliantly but in quite a different style to his female counterpart. You should be able to find this clip – information at the end of the chapter.

The music itself has a regular, insistent beat. The addition of the human voice – inevitably singing in dialect – adds an atavistic quality to the music. Schiattacore have made two CDs – not every track being a Pizzica by any means.

In the end, you simply have to witness Salento's folk music live, and even join in if you have the energy. People of all ages do participate – the children often making up their own choreography as they go along.

The Pizzica *is* Salento. It captivates and enshrines the history and the hidden spirit of the people and the scenery, evoking 'pagan' emotions from a pre-Christian era.

Youtube: To get started, try entering "Pizzica Salento BTQ (Ballati Tutti Quanti)" You will find a whole host of groups and singers with their own fascinating slant on the music – including the 'boy' dancer mentioned above. Also enter Schiattacore directly and watch their videos on Youtube and Facebook.

Schiattacore: **schiattacore@libero.it**

Francesco Giaffreda

Via Roma, 73017 Sannicola (LE) Italia

8: *Cutrofiano and Galatina*

I have come to know Cutrofiano well over the last four years; almost by accident -although chance acquaintances often turn out to be the most significant ones in life, it seems. My elder son, who tends to have greater faith than I as to my alleged ability to integrate myself into Italian society, claims that I will end up being the mayor of Cutrofiano one day. Indeed, there have been stranger individuals than me fulfilling that office during its recent history.

I had lived in Sannicola right up to 2009 without ever having even heard of Cutrofiano – even though it's only 20 minutes car drive away. Cutrofiano just happens to be one of those places to which you can all too easily become attached. It is by no means the most attractive town in *Grecia Salentina,* but it feels eminently 'liveable' in. Cutrofiano sits right on the south western boundary of this region. If you go to the attractive little town of Sogliano-Cavour, a mere two kilometres outside Cutrofiano, you have technically left the confines of Grecia Salentina. There are no obvious boundaries to this part of Salento. But I have noticed a difference in the people themselves. "Not surprising," I was told, "people from *Grecia Salentina* come from a completely different stock. Their genes are not the same."

Cutrofiano is literally surrounded by tranquil countryside on all sides. It still has bats and owls flying around at night time. I would fall short of claiming that it was hilly – like my native Chiltern Hills – but it is true to say that the countryside 'undulates' compared to most of Salento. The landscape around Cutrofiano is reassuring – apart from the fact that this area, as with much of Salento, has been blighted by a disease called Xylella, which has infected tens of thousands of its precious olive trees. Nobody is absolutely sure how this plague arrived in Puglia – and disputes are still raging as to how the disease should be tackled. The State has ordered the infected trees to be cut down to their base – including healthy trees that are within a certain radius of trees that *have* been infected. This disease has dealt a disastrous blow to Salento's main industry. The production of olive oil and wines are the region's two economic mainstays. Anger with the central government in Rome is tangible in Salento and beyond for the State's perceived ignorance and over-reaction in dealing with the threat.

So why am I so attached to Cutrofiano? Probably because tourists hardly ever go there in the normal course of events. As previously mentioned, you can reach the Ionian Sea to the west and the Adriatic Sea to the east in well under an hour by car – less if you don't want to be choosy.

It is simply a town where roughly 12 000 Salentini live out their lives. It's an 'open town'. Most of the roads are wide enough to drive along. It has a very well-cared for *piazza* where the imposing *Palazzo Ducale* is located. The municipal buildings and the surrounding edifices have been perfectly restored in traditional style and materials. It looks simply spectacular when lit up at night time too. There is a recently restored old church just off the main *piazza* – almost hidden by other buildings – which you simply must see. It is not the main church with its distinctive tower – a visible landmark for miles around – dedicated to *Santa Maria della Neve. (Our Lady of the Snow)* This little church is called **La Chiesa dell'Immacolata.** You will love it – outside and inside. Please don't miss it out should you ever end up in Cutrofiano. You will know you have found the right place because there are no seats inside the church – only frescos and a statue of San Rocco with his dog, looking for all the worlds as if they had just ambled into church as part of their daily walk around the town. I visited the church in 2018. There were no pews in it at that time – there is still nowhere to sit in 2019. A notice forbids you to take photos of the interior of the church but...who's to know, except God?

I have grown attached to this town. In one sense, it was not an accidental discovery. The university colleague and friend called Rita, whose 60th birthday we celebrated previously at the *Agriturismo Melcarne* - was fortunate enough to find a beautiful one storey stone house in the countryside near Cutrofiano. She and her husband bought the house and renovated it completely, putting solar panels on the (flat) roof and installing a completely new kitchen and dining area. The ceilings are the traditional star-shaped design – the famous *volte a stella* which is the mark of a well-constructed house in Puglia. The overall cost of restoration was eye-wateringly small when compared to what a similar scale of renovation would have cost in England. So much so, that they could afford to build a modest-sized swimming pool in the fruit and nut tree filled land surrounding the house. *Il paradiso sulla terra!* I am full of envy, by the way!

At the time of my first visit to unknown Cutrofiano, I needed to find accommodation. I ended up booking a two-week-long stay in an *agriturismo* about two kilometres from Rita's house and only one from the town centre. The rooms cost a mere €35 a night – five years ago. Meals were also available on site. I rubbed my hands in glee and booked myself in – by phone. The owner is called Giuseppe and he sounded very welcoming. However, I failed to read the web page correctly and found out belatedly that it was a dedicated "biological" establishment. That apparently means Vegan in plain English! The establishment is called *L'Agriturismo Piccapane* and it is situated on the road to

Aradeo – on a minor crossroad. Its entrance is immediately on your left as you turn right towards Sogliano-Cavour.

All I can say about Piccapane is that I was happy to stay there. Vegan food allows you to sleep soundly. Giuseppe only serves wine that is organic. I got reprimanded by him for importing bottles of 'contaminated' wine from the supermarket. He is dedicated to saving the planet whilst living in a beautiful tree-filled environment where everything grows without any chemical fertilizers polluting the soil. It was also there that I noticed that one could still see the stars at night. Should you ever decide to stay at Piccapane, be prepared for odd things to happen. I was warned that Giuseppe is an adherent of a particular form of Yoga, whose name I cannot remember, which involves giving vent to one's inner tensions by a series of vocalised cries, energetic footwork and karate-like arm gestures. The urge can take hold of one unexpectedly, it seems. I witnessed it in person after he had had a stressful day. I had to leave the room for fear of bursting out in laughter. When I saw him again this year, however, after a lapse of four years, I was hugged by him and greeted like an old friend. It couldn't have happened in good old middle-class England, I felt.

I met a host of unique Italians at *Piccapane* too; a young couple from Turin who had given up city life just to work the land for Giuseppe. They were only paid essential expenses but had free food and lodging. They also had a little girl of three who refused to say anything apart from the word "NO". I am told that she miraculously started speaking almost as soon as I left – and after I had been into the main church in Cutrofiano and lit a candle for her. Pure coincidence, some might say! Since then, they have had two more children and, the last I heard,were working the land in a similar *agriturismo* in Sardinia.

This is also where I met that delightful free spirit by the name of Doriana, whom I mentioned previously. She appears to be without any worldly ambition. At the time, she went everywhere by bicycle, even cycling to Lecce and back – 30 kilometres away - along side-roads which only she seemed to know. However, she was quite happy to accept lifts in my car when the offer was made. She would direct me down country roads so narrow on occasions that I felt duty bound to point out to her that she was NOT on her bicycle at that moment. She merely laughed and admitted the truth in my statement – and continued to leave me with the problem of extricating my FIAT Panda from single lane country tracks.

She has tried many different forms of labour since then but the routine imposed by a job involving set hours defeats her utterly. I was happy to find her back at *Piccapane* this year (2019). She is now 38 and still a free spirit who lives from day to day – somehow having failed to settle in a conventional environment. She has a journalist boyfriend, Donato, who seems to be a kindred spirit - he too working and living without a rigid timetable. They have known each other since I first stayed at Piccapane. A secret and discreet rendez-vous between the two of them took place one dark night – the effect ruined at dawn by a hasty escape by Donato pursued by the two dogs which were free to roam the estate during the hours of darkness.

Doriana has embraced the Vegan way of life utterly. She is a kind and gentle woman who would never hurt a living soul – human or animal. She lives and works to an interior timetable which is uniquely hers.

Just a kilometre away from Piccapane, on a secondary road to a town called Collepasso, there lives a couple called Antonio and Mariangela. Apart from being imbued with a profound and wicked sense of humour about the vagaries of life, they make the best pecorino cheese in the whole region – in a laboratory which is attached to their house. Do they import sheep's milk in churns which arrive from all over Puglia? No way! The milk comes from a flock of ewes which you will encounter daily as the animals are herded along the road to Collepasso by a real-life shepherd taking the animals from one pasture to another throughout the day from dawn till dusk. Antonio milks each ewe before retiring for the evening. Pecorino cheese *a kilometro zero.*

Before signing the contract for her house, just up the road from the cheese place, my friend Rita had to sign a separate contract which gave Antonio and Mariangela grazing rights on the land behind her house. How wonderful to find sheep in your garden at dawn, knowing that within a day or so the milk produced will become a rich and tasty cheese! By the way, *una pecora* is a ewe in Italian – thus the name of the cheese. *(Apologies for being pedantic – I'm sure you were aware of the word derivation already.)*

Antonio and Mariangela live in a detached farmhouse just a few hundred metres from *Piccapane* along the secondary road to Collepasso. A lot of their customers arrive in person to buy their cheese. Their fame has spread throughout Salento thanks to coverage by the local Lecce paper *Il Quotidiano. "Un sogno a kilometri zero"* – A dream at nought kilometres, states the newspaper article. Italians are brilliant at sourcing their food from as near home as possible. So remote from the English habit of selling out-of-season fruit and vegetables from the other side of the planet! "One hundred litres of milk turned into twenty kilos of cheese – every day," states the article.

It's a bucolic dream fulfilled – *ma la vita non è fiori e rose,* states Mariangela. "Life is not a bed of roses." Antonio relieves the hard labour with a very un-Italian, sharp and cutting sense of humour. Both he and Mariangela speak excellent English. While I was there this year (2019), they were filmed by an unusual couple of Lithuanians – a man and his girlfriend – who were making a video of life in Salento – commentary in English.

A and M are now helped by a young man called Alessandro – who has travelled the planet before finding his true vocation back in his native Salento, employed simply as a cheesemaker. The world is full of interesting, good and intelligent people – and they turn up when you are least expecting to find them. Antonio's mother suffers from advanced dementia, poor woman. Has she been shipped off to a home for those who cannot lead a normal life? No – Mariangela and Antonio are building an extension to their house and look after her themselves. *Viva l'Italia* – where the family still matters!

My inevitably solo appearances in this part of the world every year prompted Antonio to make some witty comment in Italian – which went completely over my head – inferring that I must be gay. Mariangela had to explain it to me. I could have protested loudly – pointing out I had two sons and four grandchildren *(The latter fact proving absolutely nothing in my favour)* Not to mention an ex-girlfriend from these parts. But I decided to play along with the banter.

"Yes, you are quite right, Antonio. I *am* gay – but only on Sundays."

For some reason, Mariangela found this notion hilarious. She must have a predilection for English humour, among all her other virtues – since she replied in like vein:

"A good job today is Saturday, Richard," she said. "Tomorrow you'll be in your element."

I appear to have a good rapport with this amazing couple of cheese-makers.

Incidentally, A and M once presented Giuseppe – of *Piccapane* fame – with a slaughtered lamb. It was barbecued and eaten by all of us - the only time I have known Giuseppe ignore the strict rules of being a Vegan. His normally healthy life style has certainly not reduced his libido – on any day of the week! He seemed to have a woman for every day of the week and a young son too, who will'inherit the earth', no doubt. *Viva l'Italia* – yet again!

* * *

What else can I say about Cutrofiano and its worthiness to be a proud town in *La Grecia Salentina?* Let's deal with that early morning coffee feeling. Well, you are spoilt for choice, naturally. There is an attractive tree-lined

138

square in town, with children's swings, an ornate fountain – but probably no water gushing forth in the summer months – and above all, shady trees. Just opposite is the *Eurobar*, which is frequented by most of Cutrofiano at various times of the day. It has a very pleasant *terrazza* overlooking the *piazza.* Nearby, there is also the *Snoopy Bar* – for those who remember Snoopy. This too is very good and does good patisserie.

But if you ever stay in Cutrofiano for more than a day, I would direct you to the *Bar Commercio,* which is situated at one end of a car park that is always empty – and free of parking restrictions. If you come in from Galatina along the straight road that leads to Cutrofiano, you can always see the church tower rising up on the skyline like a lighthouse to lead you safely home. Go straight over the traffic lights and take the first left just by the *Bar Commercio.* Park up and go and order a coffee and croissant from the owner. She has the best croissants in town. I had a croissant filled with fruits of the forest, lat June. The bar looks a bit makeshift but it is famous in Cutrofiano for being 'the' place to have coffee. You can sit outside under the trees and take your time – since you need have no qualms about car park attendants appearing inopportunely.

Just a few metres up the road into Cutrofiano, on your right, is one of the best ice cream parlours in Salento. He makes his own ice cream with proper ingredients. If you ask him a question about his products, he will delight in explaining the science behind ice cream making; a true professional – supplying a huge variety of flavours including yogurt ice-cream and soya ice cream for those who suffer from lactose intolerance. The establishment is called *DOLCE ARTE*. People go there to buy his home-made cakes too – especially on Sundays; the day when people are invited round to friends and take a selection of patisserie with them.

While you are parked near the Bar Commercio and Dolce Arte, there are a couple more points of interest to take in. The first is a machine down the far end of the car park which dispenses fresh water – sparkling or fizzy – for 5 cents a litre. People come and fill up their bottles from a drinking water supply deep underground. It tastes so much better than bottled water from the supermarkets – and helps to solve the problem of plastic waste. It is supplied by the Commune of Cutrofiano as a service to its citizens.

Cutrofiano used to have a thriving shoe industry – Italy is noted for the quality of its footwear. Sadly, I suspect their shoes are now made somewhere else in the world. But there is a well-stocked shoe emporium just opposite the water machine. It sells a wide variety of good quality footwear at reasonable prices. You have to look behind the red bars which conceal the entrance – it is not obviously a shoe shop.

Cutrofiano is also world famous for its ceramics. There are still two factory outlets on the road to Corigliano. They are both well worth a visit to see their huge selection of traditionally designed table and kitchenware - from pasta bowls to ornately coloured flower pots and serving dishes. The range of pottery on display is impressive – and of course locally made. I bought pasta bowls there for about 3€ a piece - cf English prices! The establishments are called **Salvino De Donatis** – a pottery maker since 1650! And **Fratelli Coli** – which is the first one you come to on that road. *(See their websites)*

Neighbouring Corigliano d'Otranto is also an attractive town – and has a very different atmosphere to Cutrofiano. Corigliano has a magnificent *castello* – and a railway station. I have often dropped a grateful Doriana off at the station – to save her having to cycle to Lecce. She now has a very old FIAT Panda – the original 20th century model - which often sounds somewhat reluctant to go on living. Many people still own very old cars in this part of the world – to the despair of Brussels and its Euro 6 low carbon emission engines. Many people simply cannot afford a new car in Salento, so the faithful old bangers get almost literally driven into the ground. Fortunately, the number of cars is still manageable in the rural areas of Salento.

Cutrofiano has its very own wine maker – whose plant can be visited just on the southern outskirts of the town – you can even walk there. It is called **Palamà.** It produces some excellent reds and a selection of good white wines too. Red wines are predominant in Salento – made from Negroamaro, Primitivo, Salice Salentino and Malvasia grapes. But their white and 'rosato' wines are of a very high standard too. Check opening times of Palamà on the website – or ask the locals.

Or ask the absolutely unique hotel owner – Omar. He owns and manages a modern hotel called **Naitendì** on the outskirts of Cutrofiano, just at the beginning of the road to Aradeo. The name of the hotel was invented by Omar – I wonder if you can work out how he came up with such a name? It's very easy! Among his many talents, Omar is an excellent and imaginative cook. Some of the best meals I have ever tasted have been at the Naitendì – but note, Omar will only cook for hotel guests, even if you are the only one! He is genial, very well informed, intelligent and charming. Should you ever stay there, please tell him where you heard about his hotel. It should get you favourable treatment! He also employs a delightful young lady called Sara – who is the hotel's receptionist. The hotel Naitendì was just one of those lucky finds. Omar is from northern Italy – he runs the hotel on his own with moral support from his father - a real 'family' hotel with a difference. Omar has very specific ideas about some of the inhabitants of Cutrofiano - which are gently sceptical.

I cannot leave Cutrofiano without mentioning its most notable restaurant, called *Il Borgo Chiusa*. It is absolutely unpretentious and has an extensive menu – including pizzas, antipasti, pasta dishes and fresh fish or meat. It is set in the grounds of a former *masseria (farm house)* just on the edge of the town – less than five minutes' drive from the Naitendì. The most remarkable thing about this restaurant is that it is run and financed entirely by the local council – to provide an inexpensive eating place for all the inhabitants of the town. True socialism at work! On Saturday evenings, you might have the impression that the whole of the town's inhabitants have descended on the place. It has swings and slides for children in the extensive grounds which surround the grey stone *masseria*. There is virtually no need to reserve – there must be almost a hundred tables inside and outdoors too. On Saturday nights, you feel like a member of a very large family, with at least three generations being present. It's a good place to eat – simple food and it will never let you down. That's *Il Borgo Chiusa!*

Strangely enough, Cutrofiano is not blessed with outstanding *pizzerie.* You need to go to nearby Sogliano-Cavour and look for a place called *La Locanda di Buck.* I have no idea how this un-Italian sounding name came about. This *trattoria* makes outstanding pizzas from €4 a piece – as well as having an extensive menu of starters, meat courses and desserts. It is a family run restaurant with a traditional interior with a star-shaped ceiling. Service is excellent and friendly. It is closed on Mondays – despite a notice outside which states it is open every day of the week! An oversight, obviously!

Apart from *La Locanda di Buck* in Sogliano-Cavour, there is also an excellent restaurant on the country road out of Sogliano heading towards Collepasso – and *Piccapane.* It is called *La Tenuta Pellegrino.* Just a bit more sophisticated than *Il Borgo Chiusa* and set in a beautiful rustic setting. It creatively serves a variety of simple Salento food. Furthermore, it is not expensive - certainly by English standards. But that's one of the joys of Italy. Find out where this restaurant is in the daylight – it is set back from the road and easy to miss until you know what you are looking for.

I must also mention the *Antica Dispensa* in Cutrofiano. It may sound like a chemist's shop but in fact it is a kind of house/shop down one of the main streets where a trio of doughty housewives prepare and sell homemade take-away dishes – such as *lasagne* and *parmigiana di melanzane* every day of the week - except on Mondays, of course.

Why on earth am I telling you all this - as if you are going to head directly for Cutrofiano as soon as you have landed at Brindisi? It is not my intention to "plug" particular spots in Puglia, but to persuade you that there is a whole world to explore – each place hiding its own delights and its own secrets. You will discover your own favourite towns, villages and beaches without my help. I spent years driving through a place called Collepasso – near Cutrofiano – along the main road to Maglie. "What a dowdy and depressing place," I thought. It was only when I walked from Cutrofiano to Collepasso along deserted country lanes with Rita that I realised I had never even seen the town centre of Collepasso. It revealed itself to possess one of the prettiest and spacious *piazze* I have come across – a real delight and quite different to any other town of that size in the area. It, too, has its own particular 'atmosphere'.

* * *

Before I leave you to your own devices, I should briefly mention nearby **Galatina** – just a few kilometres from Cutrofiano along an almost straight road. It is a bigger town than most I have mentioned – about the same size as Maglie. It has a railway station with regular trains to Lecce, a hospital and a maze of little side streets that have not changed for centuries. It is partly walled to the south – the town being entered via an old archway. I would advise you to explore Galatina on foot until you have sorted out the geography of the town. Some of its old streets are very narrow and you can accidently find yourself manoeuvring a car down streets never intended for anything wider that a wheelbarrow.

For me, there is one main reason above all for visiting this pleasant, friendly and lively town. Just ask the locals what the most beautiful building in Galatina is. They will inevitably tell you that you MUST go and see the church of Saint Catherine. **La basilica di Santa Caterina di Alessandria**, to give it its full title. It is in fact a few steps up the hill in a direct line with the road that leads to Cutrofiano. But leave your car along the road to Cutrofiano and walk to the church. Parking restrictions are strictly applied in the town of Galatina.

When you see the outside of the church dedicated to Santa Caterina, you will wonder what all the fuss is about. Its façade is so modest that you can have no notion of what awaits you on the inside. I can honestly say it is the most beautiful, spectacular church I have ever seen. It even beats the Santa Croce in Lecce. I think I said it already earlier on about La Santa Croce – but I shall say it again. It is enough to convert an atheist to Christianity. How powerful religious convictions must have been to create something like Santa Caterina's basilica in Galatina. Go and see this church – you will never forget the experience. Opening hours can be a bit arbitrary – you may have to call out the local parish priest. But you simply must persevere – you'll see why as soon as you step through the doors.

Oh, and by the way, there is a cute little family-run restaurant nearby called *La Tana del Lupo* – The Wolf's Layer. Not for vegetarians, I should say.

9:   *A brief digression concerning buying properties*

And now – just so you don't get the idea that I am depicting a kind of Utopia on Earth – I want to tell you about my almost amusing house-purchasing experience in July last year – that's 2019, in case you are reading this book in 2021 onwards.. It should be a salutary warning of the potential pitfalls of buying a place in Italy without reliable local knowledge to back up your dreams.

I was introduced to an entrepreneur who buys up older or neglected properties by negotiating a lower price with the owners and then renovating the property according to your specifications and budget. I trust him simply because I was recommended to him by no less a person than Omar – owner of the Naitendì Hotel. The name of my entrepreneur is Davide Mengoli and his 'studio' is in Maglie. He speaks perfect English, having lived for seven years in London, where he ran an art gallery near Putney. Obviously, he speaks Italian too – because he is. He takes care of all the legal side of house purchasing – which is far more complex than in the United Kingdom.

He is magnificently enthusiastic about what he does – and, I am sure, entirely trustworthy. I have seen a property in Cutrofiano which he has restored. You would not need an estate agent at all if you were to purchase a property through him.

But I also had dealings with a totally honest estate agent last year – and this year. His name is Antonio Magurano – also based in Maglie but he and his family live in Cutrofiano. Same applies as above should you wish to deal with an entirely agreeable and honest human being. Antonio only speaks Italian – even though he understands English reasonably well.

Both Antonio Magurano and Davide Mengoli have properties for sale, or rent, in a wide area. They are not restricted to Cutrofiano.

I have another contact in Lecce – a lawyer who will act as an intermediary between English-speaking clients and Italian estate agents or the *notaio* – the latter being the lawyer who must legally oversee any property purchase.

In general, you get a feel for people who can be trusted – even with those arch-obfuscators known as Italians! Most Italians – like most English people – are honest.

If you, unlike me, have upwards of €150 000 to spend on a house without the need to sell up in England – a dangerous undertaking in light of the current political climate – you will have a very wide choice of excellent properties in this part of Italy.

Davide Mengoli quickly understood that I wanted to see trees and have a small amount of land attached to any property which I might consider buying. But due to my 'advanced years' – or so my family try to convince me - I wanted to be not too far away from supermarkets and banks. To my joy, he had a traditional property to show me only two kilometres outside Cutrofiano – along a road I already knew.

Davide was entirely honest with me about the past history of the house we were going to see. He told me that the structure was entirely sound in all respects. It had a traditional *volta a stelle* he explained – a star-shaped ceiling. This is a sign of good old-fashioned workmanship. Ten years ago, it seems, the owner had gone beserk one day and completely trashed his own house, pulling out all the window frames, doors and the fireplace. He then ripped out the electric cables and the water pipes and taps.

The individual concerned, Davide informed me, has been 'sectioned' – yes, he even knew that English word too!

I stepped through where the front door must have been, thus escaping from the blazing hot June sunshine – which had broken all previous temperature records for the time of year. To my amazement, the interior of the house was COOL – even without doors and windows. Signor Mengoli was right in stating that the house had been well-constructed – state of the art at the time. He was quite convinced that he could buy the house and do it up within my budget - €150 000. I believe he was being a trifle optimistic. But I did not feel like quashing his enthusiasm until I had made up my mind about the rest of the house and land – which included an annexe suitable for B and B guests too. If I won the lottery, I thought, it would become a valid mission in life to restore this potentially beautiful property to its former glory.

Few country properties in Puglia have a mains water supply – the water is pumped up from the water table down below. It is often as much as 120 metres below the surface. Sewage is always disposed of via septic tanks – and gas comes via a large cylinder in the garden. The system works well – my friend Rita's country house nearby relies on all these well-established rustic solutions. They have even invented a gas cylinder which sends a signal via wifi to the gas supplier when the tank is running low.

After Davide had left me, I went to visit my friends Mariangela and Antonio – the Pecorino cheese makers – to tell them about the house I had just seen. I quote Mariangela's words:

"I have a good friend who lives in the house next door to the one you've just seen. She lives in perpetual dread and has often called out the police. The man who destroyed the house still wanders round the countryside near her house – and he often goes and sleeps rough in the house he himself burnt down ten years ago."

Obviously, being 'sectioned' does not necessarily imply that the patient is locked up in an institute – or is even under anyone's care.

I have not yet sent Davide Mengoli the text message I should send him to warn him that the situation is not quite as straightforward as he believes. I thanked the powers above that I had the benefit of local knowledge. But it *was* truly a potentially beautiful, spacious house.

With the estate agent, Antonio Magurano, I was shown an invitingly welcoming two-storey newly built house in Sogliano-Cavour which would have cost about €145 000. Friends warned me that new build houses sell easily, but the resale price tends to drop dramatically – in the same way as a new car will depreciate as soon as you begin to drive it. A salutary warning!

But, oh, I would still love to buy a house in this part of the world - when the political crisis – not mentioning the "B" word – has finally been resolved.* I would entrust either Antonio Magurano or Davide Mengoli unreservedly with the task of acquiring a property on my behalf. It is essential – especially in Italy – to be able to trust the agents you are dealing with. The contact details of both these gentlemen appear at the end of this narrative – should you ever consider buying a property in this part of the world. Their property porfolios are **not** restricted to Cutofiano, I should state again. It's just my own personal obsession that I want to live in or near this town – albeit for all the right reasons.

* It hasn't – it's worse! (2021)

10:   Loose ends...

It's simple really. I have told you all about my life in Salento over the past twenty years – because the events and encounters are real and authentic and even entertaining. But my point is that my experiences are not unique in any way - even though they are to me. Puglia, including Salento, is a uniquely special part of Italy. I know that this impression I have is shared by many other people. This book is a very rough guide as to what you might expect from its immense variety of food, wine, culture and, above all, its past. You gain a sense of history wherever you go and whoever you talk to; something which is often either blurred or over-commercialised in England. In Salento you will live and breathe its history wherever you look. Thanks to Speleo Trekking Salento, I have discovered places that would have remained hidden for ever; its beauty, its open spaces and its amazing architecture. The Salentini are rightfully proud of their heritage and do all they can to keep it alive.

I know that as soon as I commit this narrative to 'print' so to speak, I shall discover a myriad other events and places I should have included. But thanks to Amazon and e-books it is a simple matter to revise and re-submit an up-dated version of this account. To anyone who might read this story, please feel free to contact me via e-mail or the blog on my new website, if you think I have omitted any vital aspects of life over here. Equally, if you discover any aspect of the account that has changed in the intervening years, let me know.

There is no Utopia. I have tried to include aspects of life which are less attractive to contemplate. But, in general, the negative aspects are not intrusive, nor even very apparent. But the relative poverty, unemployment and the drug problem are undoubtedly a factor in people's lives. But I am sure that life in Italy has not degenerated to the extent that seems to have happened in the Disunited Kingdom. The food is so much better and cheaper too. Family life and values still prevail against all the odds. Italians are still relatively open and friendly. And they nearly all prefer Pope Francis to their current batch of politicians. Same applies in England – if I could pick a Prime Minister, it certainly would not be the present incumbent.

* * *

I seem to remember saying I would talk about Salento's wines. I realise now that the subject would require another book. I will content myself by making a few obvious comments. Whether you prefer red, white or 'rosato' *(rosé, they call it too)*, you will rarely be disappointed – if ever. For everyday drinking, you cannot do better than to go to a Eurospin supermarket where you will spend as little as €3 for a decent bottle of wine. A very successful wine producer is *Le Cantine Due Palme* – very much in evidence on publicity hoardings in Brindisi airport – does an excellent line in inexpensive wines, available in Eurospin and other outlets. Technically, *Le Due Palme* is not in Salento but in the province of Brindisi. But that is a mere accident of geography! *Le Due Palme's* regular wines are simply out of this world. They produce a red wine called *Selvarossa* which costs around €18.50 even in Italy. But it is an amazing experience.

The main red wine grapes in Salento are Negromaro and Primitivo. Salento produces more red wines than *bianco* or *rosato.* But the white wines can also be outstanding. Apart from Chardonnay and Pinot Bianco, Salento wine makers like to use lesser known native grape varieties such as Fiano and Verdeca. The most famous *rosé* wine is called *FIVE ROSES* – yes, in English - produced by a *viticolore* called Leone di Castris.

Look out for wine producers such as *Cantele* and *Mottura* – but these are just two names in a long list of excellent wine makers in Salento. A good wine shop will help you through the labyrinthian task of choosing a good wine. The Italian word for a specialist wine shop is *'un enoteca'.*

Alternatively, just take pot luck. You can't really go wrong in Salento and you will soon sort out for yourselves the wines you prefer. When in England, I raid Majestic Wine stores for wines from Puglia – where I pay three times the amount that I would in Puglia. QED

* * *

You may also remember that I said I would find out about a little monastery hidden away among the olive orchards and Cypress trees somewhere near Torre San Giovanni. It is in fact off the road which runs from Ugento to Torre San Giovanni. It will be signposted – at some point. The monastery and church are called Santa Maria del Casale – the same as the church just outside Brindisi airport. It is quite a common name for a church dedicated to Mary the Mother of Christ – it simply means *Our Lady of the Hamlet.*

* * *

I began writing this account as long ago as 2016. I suppose I got carried away with other writing projects. I have just found out that the local train company – *Le ferrovie sud-est* – no longer exists. The company has been taken over entirely by *Trenitalia,* the state-run company. There was the 'accident' I mentioned in 2016 and it seems that the *FSE* ran into financial difficulties. There seemed little point in rewriting sections of this account. Apart from some new rolling-stock, I understand the experience of travelling on these trains has not substantially changed . You still cannot be sure until the last moment whether you will be asked to change trains at Zollino when you are heading for Lecce. The only thing that has changed is that you can now buy train tickets in the main atrium of Lecce station. I trust that journeys on the former *Sud-Est* trains still have that Thomas the Tank Engine and The Fat Controller feel about them as they did for me at the beginning of this all too rapidly changing century.

* * *

I suppose it has helped me greatly that I can speak Italian. But if your Italian is shaky, do not be concerned. Unlike the French, Italians are very eager to try out their English on you. They are great communicators and will bend their knowledge of the English language into every conceivable shape in order to express the ideas they want to communicate.

I am ready to publish this book – but I suspect strongly that it will get added to and updated over time. It will become my never-ending tale of Salento. It might well appear in paperback form in the near future.

Now I have to begin the task of writing about the rest of Puglia – which will probably take up the rest of my days. The late Andrea Camilleri – of Montalbano fame – only began writing his detective novels when he was 69. Just look how much that remarkable man achieved by the age of 93.

Thank you for reading this far!

Yes, it's 2021 now – and I am pretty well stuck in the DUK whilst Covid rages all around us. Little chance of returning safely to Italy just yet, I regret to say. *Buona lettura – e buone vacanze!*

It looks as though Brexit will preclude my overriding desire to go and live permanently in Puglia. What a political, financial and cultural disaster Brexit is turning out to be! Well, many of us could see the great chasm which it would provoke. It is small consolation to be able to turn round and say "We told you so!" Well, I'm going around saying it anyway. Regrettably, Book Two may have to wait!

Richard Walmsley
Revised version – January 2021

Contact details:

Antonio Magurano (Estate Agent)

Via Diaz 2d

73024 MAGLIE (LE)

maguranoimmobiliare@libero.it

0039 0836 424299 *(Landline – please note that, in Italy, the zero is retained after the international code)*

0039 328 6712521 or **0039 346 8609067** *(Mobile numbers)*

Davide Mengoli (Property developer)

Salento With Love Srl

Via Pisanelli 17

73024 MAGLIE (LE)

info@salentowithlove.com

+39 0836 210479 *or*

+44 (0) 7956 628323

His company is also registered in England under the name Salento With Love UK Ltd

(LE) = Lecce

Srl = Limited liability company. *(Società a reponabilità limitata)*

Hotel Ristorante Naitendì – ask for Omar

Look up this site on the Internet for details and contact info which may have altered.

Contact the author: author@richardwalmsley.com

Website: www.richardwalmsley.com

You are welcome to make observations, suggest alterations via my blog.

Printed in Great Britain
by Amazon